JEAN GIRAUDOUX

The Theatre of Victory and Defeat

JEAN GIRAUDOUX

The Theatre of Victory and Defeat

AGNES G. RAYMOND

*All things can be reduced to
Aesthetics and Political Economy*

MALLARMÉ

THE UNIVERSITY OF MASSACHUSETTS PRESS

to Marshall

✦ Preface ✦

Two decades after the death of Jean Giraudoux, his plays are part of the classical repertoire on both sides of the Atlantic, and his theatre seems destined to renew itself with each succeeding generation. But while the playwright continues to bring joy to the spectator, he is still somewhat of an enigma to the literary critic. Gide, Proust, Valéry, and Claudel have a fixed place in the constellation of twentieth-century French writers, but not Giraudoux. As late as 1957, the most eminent French critic of Giraudoux's works, René Marill Albérès (*Morale et Esthétique chez Jean Giraudoux*, Nizet, 1957) called for the kind of objective information necessary to the interpretation of works that continue to baffle the scholars. "Might there be a hidden seriousness in him [Giraudoux] and is there a key to his works?" asked Albérès.[1]

Since then Laurent Le Sage, the American authority on Giraudoux, has presented a lucid and factual treatment of the subject in *Jean Giraudoux, His Life and Works* (Pennsylvania State University Press, 1959). Donald Inskip's interesting study of Giraudoux as playwright had appeared the preceding year (*Jean Giraudoux, The Making of a Dramatist*, London and New York, Oxford University Press, 1958). These studies are general, however, and do not come to grips with the actual thought of the writer as revealed by a detailed analysis of a given work. Even in Albérès's complementary thesis on Giraudoux's play, *Siegfried* (*La Genèse de Siegfried*, Paris, Minard, 1963), the critic is more concerned with the variant forms

[1] "État présent des études sur Jean Giraudoux," *L'Information littéraire*, No. 5, November–December, 1957.

than with the actual thesis of the play. There seems to be a general reluctance to study Giraudoux's works in their historical and biographical context. While the classical and universal nature of his themes cannot be denied, such emphasis throws little light on the workings of Giraudoux's mind. I have preferred to adopt a different approach to his works, to reveal how they reflect the poet's vision of reality.

The limited scope of this study calls for an explanation. In a book which ostensibly treats Giraudoux as an "engaged" writer, why omit an analysis of such key works as *Bella, Judith, Tiger at the Gates,* and *Electre?* It was not my original intention to do an exhaustive study of Giraudoux's political thought. On the contrary, it was his apparent evasion of sociopolitical problems which first struck and puzzled me, as it did so many other readers. The realization that I was mistaken and that his major themes are not purely literary came when I was living in France and was confronted with the reality in which the author lived and wrote. A conversation with the late Pierre Lestringuez, who was a close friend of Giraudoux, gave me what the French call a *fil conducteur,* the thread of Ariadne, to lead me out of the labyrinth of Giralducian mystification into the light of his rational thought. I simply followed this thread, incredulous at first, and somewhat astonished to find that research invariably verified each new intuition.

The first enigma to be solved was that of *Sodome et Gomorrhe,* that black and baffling play which Giraudoux wrote and produced during the German occupation. This led me to his posthumous work, *The Madwoman of Chaillot.* If I make no mention of another posthumous work, *Pour Lucrèce,* written during the same period, it is because it is not a political play. *The Madwoman* led me quite unexpectedly to an obscure booklet, *Les Hommes-tigres* (1926), which is classified as an ethnological study but which turned out to be a hoax of considerable proportions, worthy of a *Normalien* such as Jules Romains. This link between the early postwar period and the dark days of the Occupation suggested a hitherto unsuspected continuity in the author's reactions to the problems of peace and war. A closer examination of his first play, *Siegfried* (1928), which is based on his prize-winning novel *Siegfried et le Limousin* (1922), confirmed the indications of *Les Hommes-tigres* that Giraudoux's reaction to the defeat of 1940 followed logically on his analysis of the Franco-German problem, embodied in the mythical character Siegfried von Kleist, hero of his first political novel and his first play. Siegfried also appears in several fragmentary pieces, so that there can be said to be a Siegfried cycle embracing the period from 1922 to 1934. Thus, the subject of this book, Giraudoux's theatre of victory and defeat, is limited by its own natural unity, which I have respected by presenting the chapters essentially in the order in which they were composed. For chronological reasons, I present my findings on the Siegfried cycle in the first part of the book, but the second part follows the order of composition. The final chapter on *Les Hommes-tigres* seemed a fitting if most unconventional conclusion, since it provides the connecting link between the periods of victory and defeat. If the reader occasionally feels that he has strayed into a detective story, he is merely sharing the experience of the writer, who, contrary to all the rules of composition, found her subject at the end of her research.

This new documentation raises many questions which I have not tried to answer. In spite of Giraudoux's disdain for realism as a literary technique, he was certainly a realist in his thinking. To what literary tradition, then, can Giraudoux be said to belong? Is he, as Albérès suggests, a belated symbolist, who did for the novel and the theatre what Mallarmé did for poetry? The techniques analyzed in this study give weight to the classification indicated by Albérès, but Giraudoux also had certain aesthetic affinities with the surrealists, his contemporaries, as Le Sage shows in his book, *Jean Giraudoux, Surrealism and the German Romantic Ideal* (Urbana, University of Illinois Press, 1952). Certainly his spontaneous and intuitive representation of reality is closer to the surrealists than to the studied and deliberate imagery of the symbolists. But it is not my intention to pin a label on Giraudoux, literary or otherwise.

The reader will also look in vain for a political classification of Giraudoux. He was most certainly a *révolté,* who took a dim view of the policies of Poincaré, Briand, and Daladier. His political mentor was Philippe Berthelot, and his ideal of government was a sort of Renanian utopia, a dictatorship of the intellectual elite as opposed to the reign of the profiteers, *les gens d'argent,* as he called them, whom he believed to be the real power behind the democratic façade of government. How much of his anticapitalism stemmed from the Marxist-Leninist ideology which was rampant between the two wars and how much was based on direct observation from his post at the Ministry of Foreign Affairs, I have no way of knowing. In any event, it was a commonplace to state that wars were fought strictly for profit, and this was Giraudoux's conclusion. However, his revolt against the profiteers is not to be confused with the revolt against science and the machine. Unlike many of his contemporaries who made pious pronouncements against the evils of materialism, he was firmly on the side of progress, and he was genuinely concerned when he saw the standard of living in France falling behind that of Germany in the period between the two wars.

Can one say that Giraudoux's writings are "committed"? To answer in the affirmative, we should have to modify our ideas of the aesthetic rights of the creative artist and take a more realistic view of the restraints imposed on freedom of expression, even in a democracy. The artist, as much as the artisan, must be, first and foremost, a good craftsman. Giraudoux himself once remarked that this is the writer's principal concern, and that the rest will follow. For the artist, dedication to his craft sometimes requires breaking out of old molds to create a new one especially designed to convey his meaning. By its very newness, the art form thus evolved often obscures the conception. Moreover, the language of the creative writer is not that of the pamphleteer, though each may be trying to say the same thing in his own medium. To be "committed," a writer need not be transparent any more than the painter need be representational. Furthermore, if the writer adopts an unpopular position, the price of transparency is often suppression, in which case the writer finds himself without an audience. This is particularly true of the theatre, where, as Louis Jouvet has often said, the only problem is success, and success demands not a few compromises. "Art is always the result of constraint," said André Gide. "The great artist is the one who is exalted by difficulty, the one to whom an obstacle serves as a springboard. Art is born of constraint, lives by struggle, dies of freedom." Giraudoux spent his life in the diplomatic service, a career which imposed undeniable restraints on his freedom of speech as a citizen and as a writer. His art lived by his struggle to say what he could not say publicly and by his aesthetic aim of freeing French prose from its prosaism. In my opinion, it is not the contamination of a certain prose by poetry that has muddled the ideas of our critics, as Sartre says, but rather the debates over pure poetry and committed literature that would exclude the objective world from poetry and confuse prose and journalism, objectivity and realism.

This book is the fruit of some twenty years' acquaintance with the writings of Giraudoux, beginning with a master's essay at Syracuse University under the direction of Anna Balakian, followed by a doctoral dissertation at Middlebury College. In 1963 the Librairie Nizet published my findings under the title, *Giraudoux devant la victoire et la défaite,* which led to the present version in English, adapted from the translation of June Guicharnaud.

For this dual publication I am indebted to a number of people for their aid and encouragement: first of all, to the many persons in Paris and at Yale University, where a major part of my research was done, especially to M. René Jasinski and M. Henri Peyre; to my committee at Middlebury College, M. Vincent Guilloton, M. Claude Bourcier, and M. Jean Boorsch; to Professor Laurent Le Sage, with whom I conferred extensively in the early stages of my research and whose bibliographies (*L'Oeuvre de Jean Giraudoux* I, Paris, Nizet, 1956) and II (University Park, Pennsylvania State University Library, 1958) were an indispensable reference; to Professor Sidney Kaplan of the University of Massachusetts, who was instrumental in launching the original publication in French and encouraged its translation; to Leone A. Barron, Director of the University of Massachusetts Press, whose painstaking criticism was an invaluable aid in preparing the English manuscript for publication; and to Mrs. Doris Holden for her patient and skillful secretarial assistance. Finally, I wish to acknowledge with gratitude the financial assistance of the Research Council of the University of Massachusetts, which made these two publications possible.

AGNES G. RAYMOND

✧ Contents ✧

Introduction

The most striking feature of Jean Giraudoux's work is his style, which dazzled an entire generation. His verbal pyrotechnics are a spectacle to be enjoyed without pausing to consider what occasioned such a sparkling eruption. This style, unequaled in French literature, blinds audiences by its brilliance and enchants them by its flights of fancy, often obscuring the author's ideas. While an idea has little literary interest if it is not embellished by style, it is equally true that a writer's thought must be on a level with his aesthetics if he is to rank among the masters. The critics have customarily treated the aesthetics of Giraudoux as the expression of a moral or metaphysical concept rather than the author's vision of concrete reality. This virtuoso of language improvised on the great themes of humanity—spring, love, and war—in such a masterful fashion that his performance seems more a *tour de force* than an effort to convey an idea. And yet all his postwar works are animated by a mysterious fervor inspired as much by "adorable Clio"[1] as by Thalia. Giraudoux's art is not purely gratuitous, nor can it be explained entirely by the "alchemy of the Word." The exquisite author of *Provinciales* would have become insipid indeed if he had listened to nothing but his own sensibility throughout the years. No,

---

[1] The title Giraudoux gave to his volume of war memoirs published in 1920.

Giraudoux's art plays like the fountains of Versailles to celebrate an historic moment. This moment is certainly not July 14, but it is something similar. It is the twentieth-century drama of wars and revolutions, to which Giraudoux is one of our most eloquent witnesses.

The critics are reluctant to treat this aspect of his work. Two great critical minds, Gide and Sartre, tried in vain to penetrate the logic of his world. Gide praised him unreservedly for pulling French literature out of the mire of naturalism, but he remained bewildered before the enigma of his thought: "Giraudoux's most beautiful books were written under the sign of the dove. Not, of course, that he ignores war and keeps his eyes closed to the devastation it produces; but even in the works in which it plays a part, even the one in which it is the very subject matter, he endeavors to rob it of all reasonable significance, of all meaning, carrying all the way to paradox a thought that tends too much toward play. . . ."[2] Sartre is not nearly so generous. He notes tersely that Giraudoux has style but no ideas,[3] and this judgment of Giraudoux as a thinker has been widely accepted by a whole generation of critics.

Giraudoux's irony and intentional ambiguity make an analysis of his thought extremely hazardous. Although few critics will acknowledge that he took a vital interest in politics, one must not mistake discretion for indifference, nor humor for cynicism. Giraudoux had no taste for controversy. Consequently, he expressed himself more openly in his creative works than in his polemical writings. Since the theatre was his most direct form of communication with the public, it became his favorite vehicle for expressing his ideas. However, the richness and density of a Giraudoux text are such that the dominant themes do not stand

[2] "Tombeau de Giraudoux," *L'Arche,* No. 2 (March 1944), p. 106.
[3] *Situations II,* "Qu'est-ce que la littérature?" (Paris: Gallimard, 1947), p. 76.

out clearly. It is only from a study of the works as a whole that a pattern of thought emerges, a pattern which was not so obvious to his contemporaries, although the fact of his career in the diplomatic service made it reasonable to expect that political preoccupations would play an important part in his writings.

Such is the viewpoint of a former colleague of Jean Giraudoux in the Ministry of Foreign Affairs, M. Louis Joxe. "Indeed, a portrait of Jean Giraudoux would be lacking in essential features if a large part of it were not made up of his life as a civil servant and his meditations as a citizen. He greatly valued that aspect of himself. . . . He did not have much opportunity to translate into action the 'spiritual realism' of which he had become the interpreter, but his thinking on this point remains in the essays he devoted to French life and also in his novels and his theatre; it is here that one should go beyond the poet to find the citizen."[4] Bringing to light the thinking of the citizen behind the fantasies of the poet presents another difficulty, which M. Joxe is the first to acknowledge. At the time of this writing it is not possible to consult the personal or official papers of Giraudoux, if any remain. "I am told that it is impossible to find a single report by Jean Giraudoux, or the shortest of his dispatches . . . ," he wrote (p. 42). This lack of external evidence, while it limits the source material of the researcher, is not sufficient reason for ignoring indefinitely the influence of the poet's political thought on his writing. His published works alone supply enough information to justify a first study of Giraudoux as a citizen. Even if subsequent revelations suggest certain modifications, as may well be the case, it is time to make a beginning.

"Every work needs a context, which for writings of the past is furnished by literary history and for living writers by their own lives," said Jean Giraudoux in an early interview with Frédéric

---

[4] Edouard Herriot, with a study by Louis Joxe, *Jean Giraudoux* (Paris: La Passerelle, 1951), pp. 37–38, 47.

Lefèvre.[5] What aspects of the poet's life throw light on his political thinking? An important influence, which Giraudoux himself acknowledged in later years, goes back to the days when he was still a student at the lycée. While his family was living in the village of Cérilly, the young student had as his neighbor the writer Charles-Louis Philippe. For a French schoolboy of his generation, this was a situation comparable in our day to living next door to a television or cinema star. Giraudoux capitalized on this rare privilege by writing to him, asking his opinions on art, life, and death, which Charles-Louis Philippe obligingly recorded for him. His young admirer naively showed the reply to his schoolmates and tried to convince them to read some of the novels of Philippe. Instead of being awed by this contact with a flesh-and-blood author, these blasé youngsters mocked the literary taste and enthusiasm of young Giraudoux, thereby teaching him a lesson he never forgot: to hide his idealism behind a mask of indifference.[6]

Although Giraudoux was careful not to imitate the style or the subject matter of this obscure writer, the example of the man himself left a deep impression upon him. Because he felt responsible for the human condition, Philippe became Giraudoux's conscience, so to speak. The shadow of Charles-Louis Philippe walked at his side during World War I, and in the anguish that Giraudoux experienced when he saw another world conflict approaching, he evoked the memory of that humble writer in an

[5] *Une Heure avec . . .* (1st Ser., 1924), p. 149.

[6] This episode is recorded by one of Giraudoux's classmates, Jean-Marc Aucuy, in a booklet he wrote on *La Jeunesse de Giraudoux* (Paris: Spid, 1948, pp. 116–19). Giraudoux did not keep forever his admiration for Philippe as a writer. Actually, his writings were as far from the aesthetics of the adult Giraudoux as it is possible to be. The tales and novels of Charles-Louis Philippe treat the life of the poor with a tenderness that verges on sentimentality and with less art than sincerity.

essay published in the *Nouvelle Revue Française* in 1937.[7] The essay contains some very interesting reflections on what Giraudoux calls the bourgeois monopoly of literary expression. If Giraudoux did not try to follow in the footsteps of Charles-Louis Philippe and write for the proletariat, it was because he very soon realized that the fate of such a writer is "to become the property or diversion of the only class that has any intellectual curiosity— to be specific, the intelligentsia—and thus resound in a vacuum" (p. 103). The case of Charles-Louis Philippe was no exception in spite of his humble origins, for, as Giraudoux pointed out, the only attention Philippe ever received was from the most sophisticated journalists, the symbolist writers, the painters, and the editors of *avant-garde* journals, who paid tribute to his greatness of heart but who were confused and contradictory regarding his literary merits. In French literature, observed Giraudoux, one finds reflections on poverty by members of the privileged classes but not a single authentic expression of poverty by the poverty-stricken, save for Charles-Louis Philippe, and his heresy was turned into a literary incident which closed with his death in 1910. Thanks to this early and first-hand experience with an author who tried to reach the people, Giraudoux never had any illusions as to the effectiveness of the bourgeois writer in dealing with social questions. He realistically assumed that the only real public for his generation was the intelligentsia and that this was the only public he was qualified to reach.

This early introduction to the problems of the "engaged writer" was soon followed by an equally important contact with an "engaged scholar." While Giraudoux was preparing for the

[7] His essay on Charles-Louis Philippe was first published in the October 1, 1937, issue of *La Nouvelle Revue Française,* five months after the première of *Electre,* and reprinted in a collection of essays entitled *Littérature* (Paris: Grasset, 1941). The quotes from the essay are taken from this volume.

agrégation in German at the École Normale Superieure, which is roughly equivalent to working for a doctorate at Yale or Harvard, he studied under the famous philologist and specialist in German literature, Charles Andler. This great professor was also a critic of Marx and Nietzsche, the author of several works on Pan-Germanism, and a militant socialist until his break with Jaurès on the eve of the First World War. A man of this background could be expected to broaden the horizons of his students by emphasizing the historical, ideological, and sociological aspects of literature, but judging from the allusions to his German studies in the Siegfried cycle, I have concluded that Giraudoux was not impressed. Like all candidates for the *agrégation* in a foreign language, Giraudoux spent eighteen months of travel and study abroad, particularly in Munich, and these direct impressions of German life and culture seemed to run counter to what he had been taught in class. Despite this extensive preparation, he never mastered the German language well enough to pass the *agrégation*,[8] which may explain in part his bias against the teachings of Andler. In any event, instead of following in the footsteps of the master, Giraudoux took the examinations for the Ministry of Foreign Affairs; and in 1910 he joined the political and commercial division of the Quai d'Orsay. Meanwhile, he had published his first book, *Provinciales,* which received the approbation of André Gide for its exquisite style and perception. So it was that Giraudoux launched his career as a diplomat instead of a teacher, and as a man of letters in the effete symbolist tradition instead of in the *avant-garde* of the proletarian writers.

When the war broke out in 1914, Giraudoux was thirty-two years old. Mobilized on August 2, Giraudoux went off as a sergeant in the infantry. Instead of being dismayed by this sudden reversal of his fortunes, in the beginning, like so many others

[8] See Laurent Le Sage's article, "Giraudoux's German Studies," *Modern Language Quarterly,* XII, No. 3 (September 1951), 353–59.

of his generation, Giraudoux regarded the war as an exhilarating adventure, an escape from a mediocre era, and an incomparable opportunity to live an epic. He wrote to his friend, Paul Morand, who wanted to enlist: "As a matter of fact, you shall see such terrifying and fantastic things that one would willingly sacrifice one's right arm just to have seen them. Too bad for life as well! Everything would be so simple if only we didn't have parents!"[9]

The whole correspondence is full of wonder and curiosity regarding the great events that had revolutionized his life. Faith in tradition, the spiritual sustenance of a Barresien generation, was seriously shaken by the terrible experience of the great conflict. A few profited from the hard lesson, distilling their wisdom as they lived through the adventure of those mad years between the two wars. Such was the case with Giraudoux: sent off directly to the front, twice wounded and decorated, then awarded the Legion of Honor, he understood during those four years of war what he was later to express with his customary hyperbole—"the Franco-German question is the only serious question in the universe!"[10]

Shortly after his return to civilian life, he married and advanced rapidly in the Ministry of Foreign Affairs, where he was the protégé of Philippe Berthelot, the renowned diplomat, immortalized in the novel *Bella* as the architect of the Treaty of Versailles. Thus placed in the theatre of events where he could watch the Franco-German drama unfold, Giraudoux longed for an opportunity to express his own political opinions. He began by analyzing the situation in a novel, *Siegfried et le Limousin,* which enjoyed a certain literary success but did not provoke the debate he had hoped for. Six years later he adapted his novel for

[9] Paul Morand, *Souvenirs de notre jeunesse* (Genève: La Palatine, 1948), p. 64.

[10] See the program of *Siegfried.* See also the interview with Giraudoux published in *La Revue des Vivants,* July 1927.

the stage with greater success, but the course of events—more particularly, the admission of Germany to the League of Nations —and the exigencies of the theatre had compelled him to modify his perspective somewhat. The Siegfried cycle did not come to a close until 1934, after the advent of Hitler, when Giraudoux published the end of his play as he had originally conceived it.[11] This first conclusion, more pessimistic than that of the definitive version, proved to be more accurate and even prophetic. The Siegfried cycle is the fruit of his meditations on the victory of 1918, and it will be the subject of the first part of this study.

In addition to the Franco-German question, Giraudoux had another political concern: the recovery of France. The prewar generation dreamed of something better than going back to the old days, realizing that people in high places did not share the spirit of sacrifice which they had demanded from the country's youth in 1914–18. Giraudoux, for example, complained in a letter written to the young Morand, when the latter was spending a winter in Paris recovering from a wound:

> At the Press building, an underhand struggle between us and the journalists, who rely on the Premier, a weak, cowardly man. The whole bunch from the editorial offices, good and bad, come together in a vast hall under the august leadership of Henry de Jouvenel, who is getting fat and resembles those husbands of bawds who, in bicycle breeches, take the Great Danes out to pee. I know nothing precise about this data, which I disclose to you only in small part. But I'm becoming more and more bitter . . . about those dishonest people. We shall kill them after the war, which fortunately will have killed off a few of them. (p. 78)

It is rather a pity that Morand does not comment on these feelings, so uncharacteristic of the Giraudoux we know. However, his last words on Giraudoux are somewhat surprising: "He had the most admirably lucid mind I have ever known. In that re-

[11] *Nouvelles Littéraires,* February 6, 1934.

spect as well, he resembled the men of the eighteenth century on the eve of an enormous revolution" (p. 153). From what I know of Jean Giraudoux, I believe that judgment to be accurate, but I should have preferred that Morand elaborate on his remark.

When Giraudoux returned to victorious France, he no doubt wept like Suzanne[12] before the Inspector of Weights and Measures, for he now saw his native land in a different light, and what he saw made him wish to create for his country a modern face worthy of her past. "By 1918 the suffering, the fighting, and the sacrifice had already given them [the French people] the idea and need for a modern conscience, a happiness in practice, not the negation or caricature of it, which was all they had found after peace was made; and at the armory, where they had turned in their weapons of war, they had received nothing in return but arms for peace that were out-of-date and unworthy."[13] His reformist aspirations found expression in plans for urban renewal, on which he worked from 1918 until his death. Giraudoux's speeches and writings on this subject are collected in a volume entitled *Pour une politique urbaine,* with a preface by Raoul Dautry. In that preface Dautry mentions an early conversation with Giraudoux in 1918, in which they had agreed that

> . . . everything has made it the duty of our generation to remodel, by rebuilding, our devastated country, to make this nation that has grown old into a brand new nation in which every citizen would draw the strength and resourcefulness of his character from constant lessons of strength, elegance, and ease, inspired by the décor of life, in an uncluttered atmosphere, by daily residence in cities and houses that would be endowed with all the advantages of civilization.[14]

[12] Heroine of Giraudoux's postwar novel, *Suzanne et le Pacifique* (Paris: Emile Paul, 1921).

[13] *Sans Pouvoirs* (Monaco: Le Rocher, 1946), p. 47.

[14] (Paris: Arts et Métiers graphiques, 1947), p. 8.

This taste for perfection, this desire to create a real environment as harmonious as that in his fictional works, is far less metaphysical than it is utopian and humanitarian. Giraudoux, the aesthete, was very sensitive to the contradiction between the standard of living in France and "that total luxury which is the gift of the century." As he wrote in *Sans Pouvoirs:* "The conditions under which most of our workers and peasants live are an insult to the modern age. All the enemies that have been permanently conquered by the American worker or the Swedish peasant—the cold, the dog days, darkness, solitude, remoteness, silence, promiscuity—still hold full sway in our working-class districts and our villages" (pp. 94–95).

The reader may wonder why this question plays such a small part in Giraudoux's creative works. The answer can be found in one of his maxims on sports: "The real difference between classicism and romanticism is that the latter admits of deformed bodies."[15] In that respect, Giraudoux was a classicist, for he refused to portray in his literary works any deformity of the human body or spirit. For him the life of the poverty-stricken was not a subject for literature but a call to action. He therefore tried, with Dautry, to found an urban league, which he defined as "a body of measures by which a nation secures the rhythm and dignity of modern life," observing that on that score France was the most backward civilized country in the world.[16] The first mention of the formation of an urban league is in an interview for the September 22, 1928 issue of *Les Nouvelles Littéraires.* Questioned about his plans for a new play or novel, he answered that he had none, adding:

> On the other hand, I am busy with an Urban League, whose purpose will be to watch over the planning of Paris, the creation of

[15] *Le Sport* (Paris: Hachette, 1928), p. 18.
[16] *Sans Pouvoirs,* p. 93.

new districts. Here in our country there is almost no attention paid to city planning, and the sum of money voted for the building of new cemeteries is much larger than that allocated for new parks for children. I haven't forgotten that, before the war, I had founded a League against commerce and industry, with the same goal in mind. . . .

If the Urban League bore little fruit during those years before the defeat, the reason was less that Giraudoux was absent, as Dautry says, than that Giraudoux was never appointed to a post in the government where he might have worked to put his plans into effect. Giraudoux complained bitterly about the lack of official support for city planning in the period between the two wars:

No leader wished to understand that it was impossible for a Frenchman's soul to be enlightened and educated in a France that was falling into ruins and becoming choked with dirt. Rather, in the absence of a guiding will and vision, under pressure from big business and councils undermined by corruption, our rulers gradually allowed all supervision and responsibility to be withdrawn from the State, allowed its representatives to be repudiated, and thus left the coast clear for those in whose interest it is to put business before architecture, private developments before planning, and destruction before adaptation.[17]

A visit to Germany, where he was sent on a special mission in May 1930, increased his feeling of bitterness and made him look with great envy upon the good urban organization of Berlin, a city endowed with far fewer natural advantages than Paris:

All new Berlin, from Lichterfeld to Grünewald, is a spa without any special springs, a marina without the sea, but the idea of a holiday, which for the French bourgeois is squashed in between the heat of July and the rains of September, in Berlin is spread throughout every day, throughout every hour, and there, meals,

[17] *Pour une politique urbaine,* p. 98.

three times a day, have the charm of wealth, leisure, and—we are in 1930—some victory or other.[18]

After that visit, Giraudoux had the vague impression that the conquerors and the conquered of 1918 had changed places. The decadence of his country began to frighten him. It was perhaps during that period that he was tormented by what he called "Le Mirage de Bessines." In that curious little tale, published for the first time in January 1931 in *La Nouvelle Revue Française,* a middle-aged man, who may be the author, is obsessed by the image of his birthplace. Neither the cause nor the significance of the obsession is explained, but he succeeds in exorcising it without the help of Freud. This obsession with youth, which pervades Giraudoux's works, is doubtless the other side of the coin—the fear of old age and decadence, which was so cruelly realized by the defeat of 1940: "It would be untrue to ascribe that impression of unworthiness, which the French people experienced in 1940, to a general vice. It merely actualized collectively what a few Frenchmen had long been obsessed with individually. . . ."[19] What had been haunting Giraudoux ever since his mission to Germany was the realization that France had fallen far behind the times. He tried to dramatize that message in the first act of *Judith* (1931), in which the Jewish heroine attacks the heads of state when she discovers that the Jews are a vanquished people, whereas she had believed them to be victors. The play communicates, through the recriminations of its very bourgeois heroine, Giraudoux's fears for the future of France and his disdain for her leaders. Rereading certain scenes today, one would think that they had been written in 1940, the situation is so analogous and the tone so harsh.

Giraudoux had a profound desire to be a man of action, to

[18] From *Rues et Visages de Berlin* (1930) reprinted in part in *Pour une politique urbaine,* from which this quotation is taken, p. 27.
[19] "Discours liminaire à la Charte d'Athènes," *ibid.,* p. 114.

play a part in the leadership of his country, but he soon realized
that the role of the writer had changed greatly since the nine-
teenth century, when a leader of the romantic movement could
become a head of state and the masses honored a poet more than
a demagogue. Ideology was no longer the fashion in literature;
Barrès was forsaken by the younger generation, who had found
a new idol in André Gide, before whose complex personality
social and political issues lost all their appeal. The politicians, for
their part, were happy to keep the poets out of politics. As a
matter of fact, neither poets nor statesmen could keep pace with
the rapid march of events between the two wars. Giraudoux felt
that he had more insight than most into the problems facing
the nation, and he suffered from the lack of esteem in which his
opinions were held at the Ministry of Foreign Affairs:

> The truth is that the French State distrusts writers just as much
> as it distrusts preachers. It considers the writer to be the represen-
> tative of a particularly harmful church, that of the intellect and
> creativity, and it has broken that official bond from which its
> predecessors, kings or empresses, through their friendship with
> Ronsard or Boileau, Chateaubriand or Mérimée, acquired far
> more than even the dignity of the country, acquired their style.
> ... Thus, gradually driven out of all the offices of State, removed
> from jobs as well as sinecures, arousing suspicion in journalism,
> the writer in our country sees himself being condemned more
> and more to the role of prophet, and a prophet is, by definition
> ... the perfectly useless advisor.[20]

This lamentation dates from the end of 1934, when Giraudoux
was invited by the Université des Annales to take part in a lecture series in which the writer was to give his views on the great
problems that faced his country. He was originally assigned the
topic of women in present-day France, but he seized the opportunity to turn to a subject that was much closer to his heart:

[20] *La Française et la France* (Paris: Gallimard, 1951), pp. 21–24.

the writer and French public affairs. It is amusing to see him making the transition by equating the role of the second sex with that of the writer, who is considered unfit for public responsibility because of his so-called feminine qualities of spontaneity and imagination. He reproached the voters for having entrusted the reins of the country to politicians, so that those whom he considered the true leaders—the architects, engineers, writers, jurists, and doctors—had no authority. Just at the time when a program of public works[21] was being developed in France, the writer, he said, was being left out of the State's councils.[22]

Giraudoux himself had been banished, so to speak, to the position of Inspector General of Diplomatic and Consular Posts, so that he was truly reduced to playing the part of a prophet during the fateful years from 1935 to 1939. He never played that part with more distinction than in *La Guerre de Troie n'aura pas lieu* (1935), his greatest triumph in the theatre. At the very moment when the reoccupation of the Ruhr by the Germans was negating the efforts of the pacifists in Geneva, the play warned that war would break out, against the will of a people and despite the fine phrases of their leaders, by reason of a mysterious fatality that is not so Greek as the critics wished to believe. The identity of that malicious fate was an enigma, the key to which was to be furnished later in *La Folle de Chaillot*. One of the games Giraudoux liked to play as a child was to outwit Fate, to prevent the Trojan War, to save Desdemona,[23] but all the powers of his imagination could not change the Homeric dénouement, any more than his play could avert the catastrophe of 1940.

Giraudoux's perspicacity produced brilliant theatre, but was of

---

[21] For example, works to help the unemployed. See the *New York Times* of August 12, 1934, IV, 2:4.

[22] *La Française et la France,* p. 20.

[23] *L'École des Indifférents* (Paris: Grasset, 1922), pp. 219–21.

no use in advancing him politically. Appointed Minister Pleni-potentiary in 1933, he had still not been called to an important post when the Munich pact was signed on October 1, 1938. On October 4, Edouard Daladier, then premier, asked for full fi-nancial and economic powers to put into effect a program of general recovery. As soon as those powers were granted, he used them to carry out an offensive against the new social laws. As for a program of public works, it soon became obvious that there was none. It was then, early in 1939, that Giraudoux gave the series of lectures at the Université des Annales which we know as *Pleins Pouvoirs*. In those lectures Giraudoux spoke as a poli-tician for the first time and did what Edouard Daladier had not done—he presented a plan for the economic recovery of France. But it was already the spring of 1939. Instead of initiating a program of action, his book became, to quote Paul Claudel, "one of the most reasonable and most warranted judgments passed by an expert on the defects of a regime that is letting itself go, or to be more accurate, that is going to pot. It is a document of major and lasting interest."[24] And yet those lectures probably did accomplish their immediate objective, for on July 29, 1939, Giraudoux was named by the Daladier government to a newly created post—that of Commissioner General of Information, which André Morize, who became his staff assistant, describes as follows:

> Actually, the point was to give concrete form to some of the ideas Jean Giraudoux had magnificently expressed in *Pleins Pouvoirs:* French publishing and the circulation of French books abroad, relations with the press and the various departments of the French broadcasting system, city planning, education for the people, art exhibits, performances of music or drama, lectures and theatrical tours, the teaching of French as a foreign language, and the welcoming of foreign students in France—in short, the

[24] "Hommage à Giraudoux," Collection Comoedia-Charpentier, 1944.

presence of France in the world, including France herself—such were a few of the problems that the new-born Commissioner was to take in hand. . . . As of August 23 we got to work, and we laid the foundations for that great pacific work of intellectual and spiritual expansion. . . . The awakening was swift and brutal.[25]

On August 26 it was clear that general mobilization was imminent; the work of peace had to be transformed into an organization for war. The first task of the Information Service was to suppress the Communist newspapers. It was during this period that Louis Aragon, editor of the Communist paper *Ce Soir,* had an interview with the head of the Information Service, whom he portrays as follows:

I had found Giraudoux caught up in the machine, finally entrusted with the duties he had, in effect, spent three years soliciting, and to which ten times he had been led to believe the government was going to call him. And already finding it beyond him, lost, somewhat terrified, like an employee who has been set up in the boss's office. Already knowing that he could do nothing . . . and surprised at having to deal with censorship, which he had never believed would fall upon him.[26]

Trapped in that dilemma, Giraudoux chose to remain loyal to his post until the day Marshal Pétain, who was called on June 16, 1940 to succeed Paul Reynaud, did away with the Ministry of Information.[27]

The five radio addresses he delivered as Commissioner General of Information during the "phony war" circulated metaphors that were hardly appreciated by the French public. Angels flying over the battlefield and Hitler's black magic opposing France's white magic were not reassuring answers to the propaganda of

[25] André Morize, *France Eté 1940* (New York: Editions de la Maison Française, 1941), pp. 13–14.
[26] "Jean Giraudoux et l'Achéron," *Confluences* (1944), p. 127.
[27] Morize, *op. cit.,* pp. 17–18.

Goebbels.[28] And yet those speeches were even less pleasing to the harbingers of defeat. Though Giraudoux's efforts in the service of his country may have been clumsy, his sincerity can hardly be called into question, especially given the sarcastic remarks of a Nazi journalist, who called him "the record-holder of intelligence" because of his play *La Guerre de Troie:*

> Who has ever stigmatized that eternal old boy Demokos with more ruthless and savage perspicacity? It was awfully clever, awfully intelligent. And then, one fine day, when we were in the field, we heard blaring out over the radio old Demokos' voice itself. The old boy was explaining pompously to us that th' Jewish war was holy, that it had to take place at any price, that when it came to composing the dirges, the Intelliger vision was all there. Demokos '39 was M. Jean Giraud Jewish gang's Minister of Propaganda. He was no less than the author of *La Guerre de Troie,* but he demonstrated that, everything considered, character than intelligence.[29]

It is to Giraudoux's credit that the Nazis he but by actively participating in the Dal compromised himself not only in the ey but in the eyes of those who consider responsible for the disaster.

Giraudoux's behavior during t' dispel the cloud that hung ov friend and a member of b' prophesied pessimistically:

> He will later be repr the times in which reproached with

28 *Le futur armi*
29 See Giraudou

Information, the title of National Advisor, which he refused, and the post of Director of Historical Monuments, which he accepted, not without adding that he would bring that appointment to the attention of his son Jean-Pierre, who from the very first day had been in London as one of the close associates of General de Gaulle. Then, when the Vichy government made collaboration the condition *sine qua non* of any official activity, he officially gave up that post.[30]

In justice to Giraudoux, one must remember that the Vichy government and the Germans did their best to secure the sincere or apparent collaboration of intellectuals and artists. Even when the latter refused to collaborate, they were free to produce creative works on condition that they did not deal directly with politics. Giraudoux took full advantage of the freedom of action granted to artists. It was during the Occupation that he began to write for the cinema, and he produced two beautiful films, *Les Anges du Péché* and *La Duchesse de Langeais*. Theatre also flourished under the Germans, and Giraudoux's name was to appear on three billboards. *Electre* was revived, which pleased the Nazis because they thought they saw in it a defense of order. Then *Electre* was replaced by a new play, *Sodome et Gomorrhe,* which the Nazis understood too late to censor. Concurrently, an eretta based on *Amphitryon 38* was performed at the Opéra nique. Meanwhile, Giraudoux completed *La Folle de Chail-* which he was preparing for the Liberation.

ng with his dramatic productions, he continued to have po- interests. From his writings, we know that he took a stand in favor of the Resistance, although we have little nformation on his activities. André Beucler gives us the that he undertook, alone, to draw up an indictment war crimes. He calls Giraudoux "a recluse in refusal

nts de Giraudoux (Genève: Milieu du Monde, 1948), p. 16

the hermit of an inviolable *maquis,* a kind of liberated and revolutionary conservative, without any point of contact with spontaneous revolutionaries" (pp. 171–74). On the other hand, we know that he was in touch with Louis Aragon.[31] Moreover, according to his file at the Ministry of Foreign Affairs, he served France clandestinely. Among his political preoccupations at this time was a plan for urban renewal, for he could see the Liberation coming and doubtless hoped to play a more effective part than before the war in the rehabilitation of free France. On December 27, 1943 he published in *Le Figaro* the manifesto of the Urban and Rural League, which he had just founded and whose program he presented to the Pétain government. But his death on January 31, 1944 robbed him of his last chance to prove himself a statesman as well as a poet.

In the context of these biographical details, it would be surprising indeed if political themes did not figure largely in the writing of Giraudoux. Indeed, his political thought seems to have found its principal expression in his creative works rather than in direct action. However, apart from a novel such as *Bella* or a play such as *La Guerre de Troie,* in which the polemical subject is obvious, it is difficult to identify and analyze the political theme of an individual work. Each play or novel has its own artistic unity, but its ideology is clear only if seen in the context of the author's total work. As he himself points out:

These [works] must be considered as part of a whole and as a kind of uninterrupted chronicle of the present time. A book or a play cannot be separated from the one that preceded it or from the one that follows it. No work in itself is of any consequence. My concern is not with one book but with a series of books. The fact that they bear a title is independent of me, and around each of them I always publish five or six extensions. The same is true of our plays, numerous fragments of which are published

[31] See Louis Aragon, "Giraudoux et l'Achéron," *Confluences,* 1944.

separately after the director has found his fodder in what I bring to him.[32]

And what rich fodder he has bequeathed to the critic who follows his advice! The interrelatedness of his works and their reflection of current issues are the essential keys to his thought, especially in the absence of personal papers.

While Giraudoux enjoyed great success in his lifetime without the aid of exegeses, and there is no doubt that future generations will read and interpret his work according to their own light, the inspiration of the poet originally stemmed from his reaction to a concrete situation and a particular truth. It is not the cosmic context of Giraudoux's work which is the preoccupation of this critic. My intention is to analyze his writings in their contemporary framework, as an "uninterrupted chronicle" of his time. The process by which the creative artist transforms his vision of reality into a work of art is always a mysterious one, but the critic can throw some light on the subject by identifying the reality which serves as the point of departure for a given work. Certainly it is the first step towards a rational analysis of the author's thought.

If Giraudoux's works lend themselves to rational analysis, why is this not immediately apparent? The explanation is twofold. From the First World War on, Giraudoux's works were so contemporaneous with events that the man of letters was, as it were, a journalist, by virtue of the immediacy of his reactions.[33] His inclination to record current events ought to make his books easier to understand, and when he treats an easily recognizable situation such as the Berthelot-Poincaré case in *Bella,* or Franco-German relations in *Siegfried,* that is so. But when he tries to express what he calls "a truth outside his class," he becomes ob-

[32] *Nouvelles Littéraires,* December 19, 1931.
[33] This was certainly one of his ambitions. See p. 119.

scure, and it is not altogether his fault. Surely Gertrude Stein was right in saying that the most modern conveyances are used for traveling in space, whereas the vehicles of our inner travels are ideas that are forty years behind the times. Giraudoux, on the contrary, was one of those rare spirits who lived ideologically as well as materially in the twentieth century and who tried to forge a language suitable for conveying twentieth-century ideas. If Giraudoux's vehicle of expression often seems mysterious, it may be that our own thinking is forty years behind the times.

Giraudoux's awareness of what was new in his time was never more movingly or picturesquely expressed than in a lecture delivered at the Université des Annales in 1934:

> Today, for the first time, the great catastrophes of humanity coincide with the will of humanity to make do with its world, to get itself into shape once and for all on this planet that fell to it by chance. . . . It is no longer a question of finding supreme relief from this transitory life, but of setting up a kind of central heating and a general distribution of water, bread, and peace. Humanity no longer believes that it will change apartments in the future. So that this period of drafts, storms, and moral and physical vagrancy is, at the same time, a period of settling in.[34]

The first difficulty, then, which one encounters in analyzing the content of Giraudoux, is his preoccupation with the perpetual motion of contemporary events. This difficulty is compounded by another. We have seen that even in his lectures and radio broadcasts, Giraudoux's natural mode of expression seems to be the metaphor, especially the erotic metaphor. There are those who believe that the erotic plays such a large part in his literary universe that it takes precedence over any serious thought. Certainly the themes of love and politics are so closely intertwined that it is difficult to say which one is dominant, but what concerns us here is the startling use he makes of an erotic image to

[34] *La Française et la France,* pp. 161–62.

convey an important political idea. While Giraudoux never specifically mentions the word Pan-Germanism in *Siegfried et le Limousin,* when this student of Charles Andler calls Germany a great courtesan who flirts with the universe, we can guess what he means.[35] This association of love and politics reaches the height of extravagance or preciosity in the following metaphor, the context of which is the reaction of the Prince of Saxe-Altdorf to the revelation that his protégé Siegfried, the great statesman of the German Republic, is of French extraction. Learning that Siegfried's political enemies have discovered his secret, the Prince observes:

> For the last few years, truth no longer has had the strength to restrain itself. All you have to do is to tickle a man or a nation with the tip of your finger for either of them—and formerly it took a long embrace—to have a multiple orgasm of truths. As far as I am concerned, of the thirty family or state secrets I was in possession of when I came of age, certain of which date back to the Wallensteins, of the thirty apparently pure springs from which I alone drank and drew my right to be a sovereign, I have barely five left. You'll see. I, the oldest monarch in Europe, shall be buried with no secrets.[36]

It is not at all surprising that the reader, coming upon this passage for the first time, should stop at the image and miss an idea that is even more startling. Indeed, after all that has been written about Giraudoux's style, we must go back to the remark of Léon-Paul Fargue: "His sentences conceal a louse that jumps in your eye."[37] Thus, Giraudoux uses a preposterous image to evoke a most profound general idea. What are those "orgasms of truth," experienced today with such ease, which formerly required "long

[35] (Paris: Grasset, 1922), pp. 143–44.
[36] "Visite chez le Prince," *Nouvelle Revue Française* (October 1, 1923), p. 405.
[37] Quoted by André Beucler, *op. cit.,* p. 42.

embraces"? The Siegfried cycle refers to the events of 1919–20, when Europe was shaken by a wave of revolts against the old tyrannies, in imitation of the Russian revolution. The protests of the people, which until then had been suppressed by the tyranny of czars and kaisers, led—in a few short years—to changes that formerly would have taken decades, even centuries, of social evolution to accomplish. The Prince's enigmatic complaint takes on greater significance when we recall Kurt Eisner's disclosure, before the Socialist Congress at Berne, of documents revealing Germany's responsibility for the war. There we have one of the truths, one of the state secrets, extracted from the ruling class by an awakened people. Eisner was subsequently assassinated, and that act of violence committed by monarchists and militarists such as the Prince of Saxe-Altdorf led to the riots in Bavaria which are treated in the Siegfried cycle.[38] This new and profound political truth, that state secrets can no longer be kept from the general public, would make an interesting thesis for an historian, but Giraudoux modestly tosses off his discovery in an erotic metaphor. The idea is there, nonetheless, and reveals not only an erotic sensibility, but also a keen sense of the drama of his time.

Laurent Le Sage very rightly said that only by understanding the metaphor in Giraudoux may one truly understand this author.[39] As we have just seen, the metaphor is far more than an embellishment of the sentence; it is the sentence. Indeed, it is Giraudoux's thought become image, and such an image is so rich in associations that it is worthy of the Mallarmean tradition. It is less hermetic, however, since it holds good for the real world and for the time in which we live. The one quoted above originated in *Visite chez le Prince,* a fragment of his novel pub-

[38] *New York Times* (February 26, 1919), 1–4.
[39] *Metaphor in the Nondramatic Works of Jean Giraudoux* (Eugene: University of Oregon Press, 1952), p. 16.

lished for the first time in the October 1, 1923 issue of *La Nouvelle Revue Française,* about a year after the publication of *Siegfried et le Limousin.* Giraudoux valued the metaphor so highly
that he incorporated it in the last act of his first version of the
play, in which Siegfried is assassinated because his identity is
no longer a secret.

The discipline of the dramatic arts required Giraudoux to
make sparing use of the metaphor on stage. In his theatre the
metaphor is reduced to an ornament, and its primary function
is taken over by the symbol, which is personified in his stage
characters. "Did he not always, from one end to the other of
the large pages he filled with his beautiful handwriting, pose—
in direct or veiled fashion—the problems of France? Are not his
heroes, great and small, themselves symbols of those problems?"
asks Louis Joxe (p. 52). This is especially true of his theatre, in
which, to find the idea, one must seek the symbol. "All symbols
have their reason for being. They have only to be interpreted,"
says the Druggist in *Intermezzo.*[40] In the symbol as in the metaphor, love and politics are almost inseparable. In the play *Siegfried,* Zelten, a character who symbolizes the German revolution,
speaks of his relations with his country as follows: "They [the
generals] have just caught me in an act of adultery with Germany. Yes, I slept with her, Siegfried. I am still full of her fra-
grance, that scent of dust, roses, and blood which she gives off as
soon as one touches the smallest of her thrones. I have had all
that she can give to her lovers: drama and the power over souls"
(p. 81). This coupling, as it were, is typical of Giraudoux's
thought and reveals hitherto unsuspected correspondences between the two favorite preoccupations of the French: love and
politics.

[40] *Théâtre complet,* IV (Neuchâtel and Paris: Ides et Calendes, 1945–
1951), p. 11. (*Note:* All quotations from Giraudoux's theatre will be taken
from this edition.)

Politics often has a feminine face in Giraudoux's theatre. In four of his six distinctly political plays, the central idea is embodied in a woman: Judith, Electre, Lia, and the Madwoman are symbols of the same type as Siegfried and Ulysses. Here we confront the greatest obstacle to an analysis of Giraudoux's thought. A metaphor is hermetic, but a symbol is complex, especially when it assumes a human and feminine shape. Giraudoux was not the first to choose woman to embody an idea. Despite the gulf that separates the two writers, there is reason to believe that he drew his inspiration from one of Barrès' devices. Fernand Baldensperger wrote to Laurent Le Sage: "On a visit to Charmes, at the home of Maurice Barrès. —A copy of *Suzanne et le Pacifique* had just arrived with a dedication which should be verified and which I quote from memory: 'To the father of Bérénice, without whom Suzanne would not exist.' "[41] Compared to Giraudoux's light-footed heroine, La Petite Secousse has feet of lead, but she has the questionable advantage of being accompanied by an *explication de texte* by the author himself: "Sometimes just a simple gesture of this young woman reveals to me more serious insights into the inner life and feelings of the masses than anything mentioned in the polls of experts, the platforms of politicians, and the resolutions at public meetings."[42] Bérénice is the symbol of the masses, which Barrès studied not as a psychologist but as a politician, the better to lead them. The conscious application of intuition to the study of politics is an innovation that must have struck Giraudoux as much as it did the rest of his generation. It is a technique that fascinated intellectuals far more than it did the masses and won for Barrès at least as many disciples in the literary world as votes in his district. Even as a literary device, in the hands of Barrès it seems to

[41] Quoted in a letter to Laurent Le Sage, who has kindly given permission to reproduce this passage.
[42] *Le Jardin de Bérénice* (Paris: Plon, 1893), p. 127.

us today a curious oversimplification, but Giraudoux saw in it possibilities that he was to develop with greater subtlety and sophistication.

Giraudoux was not so eager as Barrès to interpret his symbols for the reader, but he did explain the creation of his characters in a general way. "I am surely the poet who is most like a painter. . . . In spite of myself, I write the name of each of my friends in his own handwriting, and my manuscripts seem filled with their signatures. . . . When I write about women, I observe them as I would a model; not a word about them that I found more than fifteen feet away from them."[43] There we have an admission that, above all, makes us want to go key-hunting. It is sometimes useful and always interesting to know who served as the model for a fictional character, and it will be a long time before we forget the identity of Proust's Albertine; but even were Giraudoux's loves to be revealed, everything would still remain to be said. Giraudoux portrayed his friends in the same way he copied classical subjects: they were no more than molds which served to give shape to his thought. Giraudoux did not consciously take a myth or an allegory as his point of departure; rather, he proceeded, as he said, from a specific person or a specific trait. But inevitably he saw a resemblance between the particular and an abstraction that haunted him, as in the following passage:

> Great resemblances cut across the world and leave their light here and there. They bring together, they match, that which is small and that which is huge. They alone can give rise to all nostalgia, all spirit, all emotion. Poet? I must be one; they alone strike me. . . . Miss Spottiswood walks silently alongside the nightfall, like a translation alongside its text. Were I to kiss that divine wrist, I should understand the song of birds. Were I to

[43] *Adorable Clio* (Paris: Emile-Paul, 1920), pp. 61–62.

touch my finger to those eyes, all the colors in the world would become separate.[44]

Thus, in his nocturnal stroll with Miss Spottiswood, the young girl becomes for him the symbol and the personification of the mysteries of the night.

What may easily mislead those who have followed Girau-doux's works throughout his career is the fact that the author's style and technique took shape long before his political ideas, which seem to date from his experience of World War I. As a result, his aesthetics did not change appreciably from 1909, when he first won an accolade from Gide for his *Provinciales,* until the time of his death. The evolution is chiefly in his subjects and his art forms, not in his manner. It is possible, however, to retrace the evolution of his thinking through the role of woman in his works. At first, he saw nothing in her but the symbol of a little sentimental idea. The image of Miss Spottiswood is *précieux* and Baudelairean, and it is not until *Suzanne et le Pacifique* that one sees the true blossoming of his originality. Suzanne is a marvelous tropical flower, the embodiment of the spontaneous creature, freed from the constraints of civilization by the sojourn on her island. She represents Giraudoux's inner odyssey during the six years of war. After the war the preoccupations of his personal life were combined with those of politics. It was then that Barrès' device first became useful and that woman began to play such a complex part in Giraudoux's works that several keys are needed to understand her. What will concern us here is woman as a political symbol, as she appears in *Siegfried, Sodome et Gomorrhe,* and *La Folle de Chaillot.*

Giraudoux has been accused of having skirted life, of preferring to create his personal universe. "But never does emotion flow from the heart in these de luxe works. That's it: how many

[44] *L'École des Indifférents,* pp. 69–70.

times are we moved when we read Giraudoux? . . . And how
hard-working those characters are in their sterile search for un-
happiness, which never avoids real human beings. Between his
characters and life there is the whole screen of culture. . . ."[45]
The artificiality of Giraudoux's world has irritated and per-
plexed many a critic, but if Giraudoux has taken the liberty of
screening from his work most of the absurdity and indignity of
the human condition, so much the better, perhaps. Twentieth-
century man does not leave a flattering image of himself in the
literature of our time. The screen of culture is all that dis-
tinguishes him from the beast. Emotion does, in fact, play a part
in Giraudoux's works, but not in the limited sense. It stems
from a resemblance between men and events which moves
us more than the fate of his individual characters. The main-
spring of emotion in these courteous and *précieux* souls is the
drama of our time, which gives a resonance to his works that is
difficult to define. Its effect is partially subliminal. We are moved
without knowing precisely why or by whom, for Giraudoux's
art is not purely intellectual. Beneath the elegant banter we detect an undercurrent of gravity without being sure of its source.
The idea is there, however, Sartre notwithstanding, and it lends
itself to analysis.

[45] Marie-Jeanne Durry, "L'Univers de Giraudoux," *L'Arche,* No. 2
(March 1944), p. 118.

After the Victory

THE SIEGFRIED CYCLE

Siegfried et le Limousin

Until the publication of *Siegfried et le Limousin* in 1922, Giraudoux's writings were known and appreciated only by the happy few. His publisher, Bernard Grasset, was determined to make this promising author known to the general public. It was with this in mind that he reportedly instigated the founding of the Balzac prizes by Basil Zaharof.[1] In any event, the two novels which were selected to receive the first awards were both published by Grasset. Out of three hundred contestants, a jury presided over by Paul Bourget chose *Siegfried et le Limousin* by Jean Giraudoux and *Job le Prédestiné* by Emile Baumann. At a time when the vogue of literary prizes was just beginning, such an award assured the author of almost worldwide renown. *Siegfried et le Limousin* was translated into most European languages, and Giraudoux's name was prominently displayed in the windows of major bookshops.

One critic dismissed Emile Baumann's novel as a bad writer's worst book,[2] and literary history has not disproved that judgment. On the other hand, *Siegfried et le Limousin* introduced an author whose fame was to grow steadily with the years. To the pedestrian prose of the realist writer, Baumann, Giraudoux op-

---

[1] I received this information from the late Jean Marx, a colleague of Jean Giraudoux at the Quai d'Orsay.

[2] Albéric Cahuet. *Illustration* (November 11, 1922), pp. 468–69.

posed a literary technique that obscures both the flaws of composition and the content of his own novel, which compelled recognition largely by its style. It is essentially the same style which Gide had praised in Giraudoux's first work, *Provinciales*. There is a perceptible change, however, in tone and subject matter. His first books are distinctly narcissistic, betraying a secret nostalgia for that freshness of vision which is peculiar to childhood and primitive man. The experience of the great conflict of 1914–18 caused Giraudoux to turn his attention outward and forward. In his war memoirs he achieved a more objective vision of reality, with only traces of nostalgia. In the postwar period the tone of his writings became gayer with *Elpénor* (1919) and fairly bubbled with the joy of living in *Suzanne et le Pacifique* (1921). But it was not until *Siegfried et le Limousin* that he was to exteriorize, as it were, and take his inspiration from the great events that convulsed Europe in the wake of the First World War.

This novel is a curious reaction against two trends current at the time: the novel of confession, which Gide's success had popularized, and the prosaism of the naturalist writers. Giraudoux's natural delicacy and reticence led him to veil his personal revelations in symbolic form, impersonalizing the autobiographical content of his writings even when they are in the first person, as is the case with *Siegfried et le Limousin*. This reticence is accompanied by a droll humor which pervades the work, making it difficult for the reader to know when to take him seriously. While the novel contains reminiscences of the author's student days in Munich, its principal subject, as the title indicates, is the political situation in postwar Germany as seen through the eyes of a Frenchman (le Limousin is the name of Giraudoux's native province). Giraudoux may have intended this work to be a twentieth-century contribution to Balzac's *Comédie humaine,* but he had no intention of adopting realistic techniques. "I in no way appreciate realist literature," he said in an interview, adding that he liked Jules Renard as he would an alphabet.[3] But if to the techniques of realism he opposed a technique that has no label in the literary manuals, this does not mean that his thinking was not realistic. On the contrary, it was so realistic and so topical that his literary antirealism was often a convenient mask.

Siegfried et le Limousin is at once a pamphlet and a stylistic exercise, an attempt to transform a journalistic account of current events into a modern saga. On a first reading, the plot of the novel is easily lost amidst the welter of recollections, anecdotes, and descriptive passages—all highly diverting because of the lively wit and imagination of the author. The narrator of the story is Jean, who is presumably the author's mouthpiece. Jean is puzzled by the articles of a writer for the *Frankfurter Zeitung,* who signs with the initials S.V.K. Certain passages remind him of Jacques Forestier, a French journalist he once knew, who was listed as missing during the war. The arrival in Paris of Count von Zelten, a former acquaintance from Munich, offers a possible solution to the mystery. Zelten, whom Jean had met during his student days before the war, had always embodied for him all the charm and fantasy of the German Romantics as well as their generosity. Zelten informs him that the author of the articles is Siegfried von Kleist, one of the leading dialecticians in Europe and a critic of the Weimar Constitution. Siegfried's story is a singular one. He was picked up by the Germans on the battlefield, naked and at the point of death. When he recovered consciousness two months later, he had lost his memory and had to be completely reeducated by his German captors, who concealed his French origin. In a short time, he had become a well-known jurist and statesman.

The first meeting between Jean and Zelten takes place in Paris at the Café de la Rotonde. Subsequently, both men leave for

[3] Frédéric Lèfevre, *Une Heure avec . . .* (1st Ser., 1924), p. 151.

Munich, Jean in order to look up Siegfried, and Zelten to lead a revolution. Jean finds lodgings near Siegfried in order to observe him. He soon becomes convinced that Siegfried is Forestier, and he seeks an occasion to meet him. On learning that Siegfried is looking for a French tutor, Jean applies for the job and becomes part of Siegfried's entourage. But in spite of Jean's constant companionship and his subtle attempts to evoke the past, Siegfried shows no flicker of recognition. Meanwhile, Zelten has his revolution, which is short-lived; but he brings about Siegfried's downfall with his own by denouncing him as a foreigner. Thus Germany loses the two men who sought to direct her destiny and who represent in a symbolic manner the forces vying for control of the country.

Jean is witness to all these events. He is threatened by Siegfried's fanatic supporters, Eva von Schwanhofer and Professor Schmeck, and imprisoned along with the leftist fanatics such as Lieviné Lieven. He is also in contact with Zelten's former wife, Geneviève Prat, a French sculptress whom he knew in Paris and who suddenly appears in Munich. She is apparently in league with Jean and Zelten to help Siegfried recover his memory and return to his French past, but she dies inexplicably at the height of the political drama, leaving her French heritage to Siegfried. There is no further mention of Zelten, who disappears from the scene after his denunciation of Siegfried. The latter has been carried off by Eva to her villa at Oberammergau, where Jean eventually locates him. Siegfried rushes off with Jean to Geneviève's deathbed, then boards a train for France. His reaction to his fall from power is developed very sketchily in a letter he writes to the Prince of Saxe-Altdorf explaining his hasty departure. The letter slips out of Siegfried's pocket into the hands of Jean as the latter rides with his sleeping friend across the Franco-German border. On reading the letter Jean learns why Siegfried was allowed to leave the country alive: an agreement had been reached, presumably with Eva and Schmeck, to cover his disappearance by a false report of his death by drowning. As the novel ends, Siegfried is still asleep and ignorant of the details of his past, which Jean is about to reveal to him.

This somewhat disjointed plot has been thrown together in the most cavalier manner imaginable. In the interview with Frédéric Lefèvre in which Giraudoux expressed his disdain for realist literature, he admitted having written *Siegfried et le Limousin* in twenty-seven days without any preconceived plan, inventing both the plot and the characters as he went along.[4] The discerning reader can perceive the unity of theme indicated by the title, but the order of events is no more logical than that of a dream sequence or of automatic writing.

The critics greeted the work by paying tribute to its literary qualities, but they avoided any analysis of the content of the novel. They pointed out in a general way the contrast between France and Germany, which the author evoked with subtle irony in the portrayal of his characters; but they tended to see Giraudoux merely as a brilliant writer, who treated a current topic with more whimsy than seriousness. If he had not pursued the subject any further, this view would have been justified. But the myth of Siegfried was to haunt Giraudoux for a long time to come. It was the subject of his first play and of many short pieces that continued to appear until 1934. It deserves further study, for the play *Siegfried* is an important landmark both in the history of the theatre and in Giraudoux's career.

Although no critic to my knowledge has spelled this out, *Siegfried et le Limousin* is an historical novel whose context can be found in the newspapers of the period. Its contemporary relevance is made clear in the opening lines, but the author's chronology is so confusing that it is little wonder that the critics have been reluctant to discuss the plot. The novel was published in Novem-

[4] See pp. 32–33, 65.

ber 1922, and so its first sentence, "The time was January 1922," seems to establish not only the date of its dramatic action but also the date of composition. But such is not the case. The opening sentence deliberately puts the reader on the wrong track because it does not cover the historical events of the novel; and the third sentence raises a serious question as to the date of composition by alluding to a series of international economic conferences which took place between January and June 1922: "But the diplomats were still wearing themselves out placing, under sunny skies and foggy skies in turn, at Cannes and then at Boulogne, at Genoa and then at the Hague, a keystone for Europe." This sentence alone covers a six-month period, bringing the events of that first page startlingly close to the date of publication. It suggests that Giraudoux began writing the novel in January 1922 and sent it to press in June of that year, inserting this last sentence in the final draft or on the proofs. This does not necessarily contradict his statement that he wrote the novel in twenty-seven days. Nor does it prove that he actually did compose the novel in the six-month period directly before it went to press.

Giraudoux may have chosen the January date for historical reasons that had nothing to do either with the economic conferences or with the date of composition, since he insisted upon the month of January as the starting point for the action of his play *Siegfried* even though he changed the year to 1921 and the place from Munich to Gotha. The chronology of these opening lines does not establish anything more than the author's intention to impress the reader of 1922 with the contemporaneity of his subject. This is reinforced by Jean's even more startling allusion to yesterday's headlines: "Each day I read the German newspapers, in the hope—which as a matter of fact was always disappointed—of finding a word, one single friendly word directed to a Frenchman, even international Frenchmen such as Jeanne d'Arc and Cachin, or to a region of France. . . ." The juxtaposition of the Maid of Orleans and the Communist deputy who had convinced the French socialists to join the Third International must have astonished the reader at a time when the newspapers saw Communist conspiracies everywhere. This strange parallel, typical of Giraudoux's love of paradox, is the author's oblique way of expressing his concern over the deterioration of relations between France and Germany and the *rapprochement* between Germany and Soviet Russia.

Early in 1918 an event took place which the Allies considered more menacing to their safety than the onslaught of the German armies. The Russian Revolution, followed by the Treaty of Brest-Litovsk, dealt a hard blow to the Allied cause. France, in particular, as the world's banker, saw herself threatened by the fall of the Czarist government, of whom she was the largest foreign creditor. It was then that Clemenceau ordered several divisions of the Eastern army to turn toward the Ukraine instead of entering Germany; and as soon as the armistice with Turkey was signed, he sent the French fleet into the Black Sea "to accomplish the encircling of Bolshevism and to bring about its downfall."[5] But the soldiers and sailors, weary of making war and sympathizing with the Russian Revolution, rose up and put an end to French intervention against the Soviet Republic. The other Allies had no more success: the first intervention against Bolshevism was a complete failure.

The Black Sea rebellion and the triumph of the Russian Revolution had great repercussions: the entire French economy sustained huge losses; a schism in the Socialist Party was brought about by the organization of the Third International; the brilliant defense of the Black Sea mutineers, led by Marcel Cachin before the Chamber of Deputies, found many sympathetic ears among workers and intellectuals. In 1919, hope was mounting in revolutionary circles, whereas the bourgeoisie was watching

[5] *Le Matin,* September 17, 1922.

the future with anxiety. Meanwhile, commerce was flourishing again on the international level, and the race was on to find new markets. In April 1922, England undertook to organize the economic recovery of Europe by calling together the Western countries, including Russia and Germany, at the Geneva Conference. The avowed objective of the conference was the revival of trade throughout the world. That particular conference was the most significant of the series mentioned by Giraudoux at the beginning of his novel, since it revealed the true character of that "keystone" which was being sought for Europe. The great hope of all the European countries, except France, was to arrive at an economic and financial agreement with the new Soviet Republic which would extract with money the concessions they had not been able to obtain by means of arms. France imposed one condition as a prerequisite for the resumption of any trade relations: Russia must pay all state debts contracted by the Czarist government. Poincaré's intransigence on that point was matched by that of the Russians, who answered by presenting a bill for damages caused by the Allied intervention in the civil war. At the end of five weeks of debate on questions of principle, Germany and Russia signed an agreement mutually renouncing all state indebtedness, as if to give the rich Allies a lesson in generosity. This agreement, known as the Treaty of Rapallo, brought sharp protests from France, in particular; in point of fact, an understanding between Germany and Russia was the last thing the Allies had wanted. In Germany as well, there was a great deal of opposition on the part of the old regime to the Republic's foreign policy. That opposition resulted in the assassination of Walther Rathenau, Minister of Foreign Affairs and signer of the Treaty of Rapallo, which occurred on June 24, 1922, a bit too late to have any influence on the composition of *Siegfried et le Limousin*. Such was the economic and political climate of the times, which Giraudoux evoked by the mere mention of Genoa and Cachin.

A short piece entitled "Le Signe," which appeared in the July 1922 issue of *Les Ecrits Nouveaux* and which Giraudoux republished in part in *Siegfried et le Limousin* (pp. 10–11), gives us some insight into Giraudoux's reaction to social change. It has to do with the untimely death of a certain Dumas, who was well known in the industrial world for his steel works and his patents. Dumas had one very special quality, which the narrator describes as follows:

> Multimillionairesses and madwomen found it astonishing that they adored him even though he was small, bearded, and sarcastic, but it happened that any unemployed workman they met in the street, any poverty, and by analogy, any injustice, accident, mutilation, and eczema they caught a glimpse of, was bound up in their thoughts with Dumas by a kind of rainbow, the rainbow Dumas no doubt, who absolved their idleness, their beauty, and all their luxuries.[6]

We see here a certain irony with regard to heiresses and madwomen, but the role of Dumas is not very clear.

Dumas' death made the narrator inexplicably sad, though not for personal reasons: "What I felt, in effect, was what the war had spared me: the impression of defeat. I had lost an unknown game, I had had my wealth and invisible provinces amputated . . . " (p. 151). The narrator awaits some sign from man or nature to restore his faith in the future. At the end the sign is given, but he does not explain how or by whom. Dumas' death is obviously a symbol, but of what? Without knowing exactly who Dumas was, we do not understand the narrator's neurasthenia. Dumas is a portrait of a wealthy industrialist, Achille Fournier, who before the war had been a penniless young man.

[6] "Le Signe" was republished in *La France Sentimentale* (Paris: Grasset, 1932), p. 140, and the quotations are taken from this edition.

Although extremely well educated, he had gone to work for Le Creusot, France's most important iron and steel works, instead of entering the professions. He began as a clerk in the legal department, and in less than ten years rose to the rank of director general of the enterprises. He was regarded by his empolyers and the multimillionairesses as the ideal laborer, who worked for the joy of working and did not envy the wealth he was producing for others. But Fournier died, at the age of thirty-seven, a sudden and dramatic death, which the journalist Jean de Pierrefeu relates in the following manner:

> One night as he was being driven toward one of the factories which he ran—that is how he spent four nights out of seven, sleeping in the car to save time—his auto arrived at a railroad crossing that was barred. At the shriek of the horn, the attendant, half asleep, rushed up and pulled open the barrier. Just as the auto began to cross the tracks, the motor stalled. Before the chauffeur had time to start off again, there was a clap of thunder, and in a double flash, the express passed by. . . . Perhaps the locomotive that killed him came from one of his own ironworks. One can imagine him visiting the shop, his hand stroking the shining rump of the monster.[7]

In Giraudoux's account Dumas apparently committed suicide by diving into a stream, and his body was never found. This time reality is more ironic than fiction. Jean de Pierrefeu heightens the drama by describing the despair of the president of the company, Mr. Schneider, kneeling beside the deathbed of the young genius: "I had the vision of a king at the deathbed of his prime minister and fearing for the dynasty" (p. 177). In order to realize why the death of Fournier left such an impression on Giraudoux and Jean de Pierrefeu, one must recall the Marxist tenet that capitalism bears within itself the seeds of its own destruction. To many people in the early postwar era, the death of

[7] *L'Anti-Plutarque* (Paris: Plon, 1925), p. 176.

capitalism and bourgeois democracy seemed imminent, and it is this fear which Giraudoux evoked in relating the death of Fournier, which impressed him as a sinister omen.

How the death of Fournier is linked with the Franco-German problem is another question. It would seem that it also played a role in the creation of Giraudoux's mythical character, Forestier-Siegfried. In the novel Dumas-Fournier is mentioned in a manuscript written by Jacques Forestier which is later plagiarized by S.V.K. in an article in the *Frankfurter Zeitung*. Later on in the Siegfried cycle, certain details of this passage appear in a fragment describing Forestier, instead of Dumas. "You know what Forestier was to us. He was our leader. At thirty he ran the largest factories in France. . . . Out of 5,313,000 tons of steel produced in France, his factories were responsible for 3,800,000. He left when war was declared and disappeared at the very start. No trace of him was ever found."[8] The economic power represented by the French industrialist, Achille Fournier, has thus been transferred to Forestier-Siegfried. This identification of Fournier with the amnesic soldier Forestier appears in more indirect ways in the novel. It is significant that Giraudoux relates the death of Forestier and that of Dumas on the same page, but in both cases he treats their death as a disappearance, which permits him to transplant them to Germany in the guise of his mythical character Siegfried. As Jacques Forestier, the French journalist, Siegfried has another counterpart in real life. He is André du Fresnoy, a contemporary of Giraudoux who was killed in action on August 22, 1914, and to whom Giraudoux dedicated two volumes of his war memoirs. According to Paul Morand in his *Souvenirs de notre jeunesse* (p. 138), André du Fresnoy earned his living by writing during the day for *L'Action Française,* a newspaper of the extreme right, and for a socialist paper at night, a detail which Giraudoux alludes to in the novel. In

[8] *Théâtre complet,* XII, *Variantes,* I, p. 162.

fact, it was a memorial service for André du Fresnoy which apparently inspired the idea of reviving both the journalist and the industrialist in a work of fiction (p. 10). A further biographical inspiration, the amnesic soldier, can be traced, as Albérès has suggested in *La Genèse de Siegfried,* to the war experience of Giraudoux's brother, who suffered from amnesia (p. 18). Thus, the French origins of Siegfried reveal the curious synthesis of an unbiased or opportunistic French journalist who died on the field of battle, a brilliant young industrialist who also died in action, so to speak, and the phenomenon of the amnesia case produced by the horrors of war.

While these biographical sources throw some light on the genesis of the novel and on the creation of Forestier-Siegfried in particular, they have little bearing on the political crisis evoked in the conflict between Siegfried and Zelten. Again it is necessary to return to the historical background of this troubled period. Despite the first sentence of the novel, Zelten's revolution refers to events which transpired not in 1922 but in the spring of 1919. While France was trying to crush the Russian Revolution, there were insurrections on the other side of the Rhine that nearly brought Germany into the Soviet camp. A first revolution in 1918 had overthrown the monarchy and brought victory to a coalition of moderate Socialists, Independents, and Spartacists. That coalition set up a provisional government headed by Friedrich Ebert as Chancellor, while awaiting the election of a Constituent Assembly and the adoption of a republican constitution. The Independent Socialists and Spartacists, under the leadership of Karl Liebknecht and Rosa Luxembourg, refusing to stop there, tried to establish a dictatorship of the proletariat, as in Russia. Early in January 1919 the partisans of Liebknecht rebelled against the Ebert government. Liebknecht and Rosa Luxembourg were assassinated by members of the army at the end of a week of violence. The elections took place, and on July 31,

1919, the National Assembly adopted the Weimar Constitution, signed the Treaty of Versailles, and elected Ebert President of the German Republic. It is with this series of events that Siegfried is associated as the principal proponent of the Weimar Constitution.

In the south of Germany the Bavarian Republic went through a similar crisis. The government of Kurt Eisner, which leaned toward moderate socialism, was the object of a royalist conspiracy. On February 22, 1919, Kurt Eisner was assassinated by Count Valley Arco, a member of a secret society of aristocrats and officers. That counterrevolutionary crime set off a series of communist riots in Bavaria, which were crushed by Noske's troops in the month of May. It is one of these uprisings which Giraudoux evokes in *Siegfried et le Limousin*. The time and place of the dramatic action can be established by Zelten's *coup d'état,* which Giraudoux calls "the second Bavarian Republic" (p. 237)—that is to say, the Soviet Republic proclaimed on April 7, 1919, one month after Eisner's death. This is further borne out in the first version of the play when one of the characters points out the place where Eisner fell, assassinated, *one month ago.*[9] Siegfried's role also suggests that of Hoffmann, whose parliamentary regime had succeeded Eisner's. The Hoffmann government came back into power with the help of Noske, and on August 14, 1919, Bavaria in turn adopted a republican constitution. Thus, before the end of that fateful year, Germany apparently began moving in the direction of democracy, but those who knew the country well were far from being reassured by that bloody victory over Bolshevism. From the moment the peace was signed, the Allies were distrustful of the new Republic, fearing a rebirth of German imperialism; but since they feared the spread of Bolshevism even more, they supported the new regime.

[9] *Siegfried von Kleist, Théâtre complet,* XII, *Variantes,* I, p. 14.

Giraudoux saw Germany as a country which was almost equally divided between the extreme right and the extreme left. At best the German Republic could establish only a shaky balance between these two forces since it had as yet no real roots in the country and was primarily a government imposed by the victorious Allies. Giraudoux feared that the German militarists would use the Republic as a screen behind which to prepare a war of revenge. Thus Siegfried, the German statesman of French origin, is a symbol of the German Republic, born, as the name suggests, of the Allied victory and peace. Zelten represents the forces of the extreme left, which are indigenous to Germany but which are unacceptable to the Allies.

The political opposition between Siegfried and Zelten can be explained in more specific terms by identifying them with their German prototypes. In addition to the three French models which we have already cited for Jacques Forestier, there are as many more for his Teutonic counterpart, Siegfried von Kleist. The first two are obvious. Named for the hero of the *Ring des Nibelungen,* who was also ignorant of his origins, Siegfried is the protégé of the big German industrialists, Stinnes and Wirth, who, like the dwarf Alberich, want to use his strength to win back what might symbolically be called the Rheingold.[10] As for Siegfried's family name, von Kleist, Zelten explains that it was given him in remembrance of the great German poet because the bullet that took Kleist's life and that which took away Siegfried's memory penetrated in exactly the same place.[11] Behind this jest there are real points of analogy, Kleist having been, like Siegfried, at once a poet, a soldier, a philosopher, and a jurist.

[10] For the political symbolism of *The Ring,* see George Bernard Shaw, *The Perfect Wagnerite.*

[11] *Siegfried et le Limousin* (Paris: Grasset, 1922), p. 130. All quotations from the novel are taken from this edition.

The third and most significant German model for Siegfried was a contemporary figure whose portrait was sketched by Ambroise Got, a journalist attached to the French military mission in Berlin from March to July 1919. Got was witness to the Spartacist rebellions in Bavaria and seems to have known all the major figures involved. He recorded his impressions in a book entitled *L'Allemagne après la débâcle,* published in Strasbourg in December 1919. This was followed by another volume in 1922 entitled *La Terreur en Bavière,* which treats the same subject and whose chief interest lies in a series of biographical sketches of the main instigators of the Bavarian revolution. Here we see portrayed in another light several of the characters who appear in *Siegfried et le Limousin.* Both books contain so many details which are identical or similar to those found in the novel that there is reason to believe that Got's report was an important source. Certainly this reporter was known to Giraudoux, for the name of Ambroise Got appears in the novel (p. 240). On the other hand, it is not impossible that Giraudoux himself could have been a witness to the events that he describes, though not in any official capacity, for we know that he was demobilized on March 29, 1919, and reinstated in the service of the Ministry of Foreign Affairs on May 15, 1919.

Among the moderates whom Ambroise Got portrays in *L'Allemagne après le débâcle* is Professor P. W. Foerster, who bears an unmistakable resemblance to Forestier-Siegfried. Although a Prussian and a Berliner, Foerster was nevertheless against Pan-Germanism and rejoiced at the Allied victory. His father had been one of the most active members of the pacifist movement before the war. Foerster himself was a philosopher, a Social Democrat, and a well-known Francophile. At one time he was even a candidate for the presidency of the German Republic. The day after the Bavarian revolution, Eisner asked Foerster to represent the interests of Bavaria at the international socialist conference at Berne. Foerster served loyally, refusing any compensation; but following the adoption of the Constitution of the German Reich, he became disillusioned and retired from active politics.

Foerster disapproved of communism, the centralization of Germany, and the Treaty of Versailles. He feared both the extreme right and the extreme left and would have liked to see the Allies occupy Germany to provide a bulwark against this dual menace. As a permanent solution, he favored a series of autonomous republics to prevent the Prussification of the Reich. Ambroise Got, in 1919, described him in the following words:

> Today he must be getting on toward fifty. Seeing him so alert and with such a youthful expression, one would not think he was over thirty-five, he has been so preserved from all blemishes by the sobriety of his life and the purity of his habits. A light brown beard, with a few silver threads mixed in, lengthens his oval face, tanned by fresh air and movement. Very gentle eyes, which inspire confidence, light up this handsome face. . . . He is not a doctrinarian, and in that he differs from his German fellows. He has not created any great system, and in that he is closer to us. His is a Latin mind, a clear brain. He is not endowed with that sense of geometry he attributes to his compatriots, but rather with that sense of finesse with which he likes to grace the French. . . . I rather think he himself must recognize that most of his compatriots, blinded by the cult of strength, do not understand him and directly refuse him the right to call himself German. (pp. 246, 250)

To crown the resemblance to Forestier-Siegfried, Ambroise Got informs us that he met Foerster by giving him French lessons (p. 245), a detail which recalls how Jean succeeded in obtaining an introduction to Siegfried. It would seem, therefore, that this portrait of F. W. Foerster suggested much more to Giraudoux than Siegfried's French name, Forestier. This Latin brain in a

German head, this champion of a republican form of government, this sponsor of the Weimar constitution, this Francophile who is rejected by his people as if he were a foreigner, this philosopher who takes French lessons is obviously one of the models for Giraudoux's hero.

In the eyes of Ambroise Got, Professor Foerster has all the qualities of the ideal German and is the Allies' best hope for a lasting peace. However, in creating Forestier-Siegfried, Foerster's fictional counterpart, Giraudoux does not evaluate his role in the same manner. He sees lurking behind the innocuous façade of this honest bourgeois statesman and philosopher sinister forces that make use of idealism to attain their own ends. These forces are depicted by Giraudoux in the person of Siegfried's nurse, Eva von Schwanhofer, and her cohorts. It was Eva who gave the amnesic soldier his first image of his new country and who taught him to use the German language. She had been chosen for the task because she corresponded most precisely to the model woman described in the circular of a certain medical officer, whose racist ideas anticipated the Nazis. But Siegfried is not her only pupil. She is president of an association of young German girls who recite a formula that begins as follows: "O Germany, we swear that we will have five sons to avenge you. The first will wreak vengeance on the Poles, who are an insult and a mockery to Europe. The other four will wreak vengeance on the French, who deprive existence of all value" (p. 165). To her small cousins she taught the invocation which all well-born Bavarian children recite kneeling at their bedside: "Saint Mary, Mother of God, deliver us from the horrible race of Frenchmen" (p. 161).

Eva sends a professor and a baron, both organizers of extremist groups, to dissuade Jean from revealing what he knows about Siegfried's identity. Siegfried is needed, they say, whatever his nationality, to pass judgment on the plans for a republican constitution. These men, representing the forces of hate and reaction, are counting on Siegfried's lucid brain to form a government that will protect their interests while at the same time allaying the suspicions of the Entente. Siegfried's amnesia symbolizes the Allies' forgetfulness of the past. This amnesia, as Giraudoux so aptly characterizes the policy of the Entente, combined with a blind idealism, permits Siegfried to become the tool of the same classes of German society whose unbridled ambition led to the First World War. Since Siegfried and the rest of the world do not see that the German Republic is being used by these forces to mask their preparations for a war of revenge, the peace of Europe will be short-lived.

In contrast to Siegfried, Giraudoux presents another idealist in the person of Count von Zelten, who opposes the militarists and the industrialists who are supporting the Republic. Zelten derides the Siegfried plan, that is to say, the adoption of a republican constitution, which he finds as practical as making the dragon of the Wagnerian hero swallow an alarm clock in order to teach him to tell time. It is Zelten who makes the very perceptive analysis of the basic differences between the two countries (pp. 32–34), and it is he who cautions the French against the soul of a people motivated by delusions of grandeur. Zelten, however, is portrayed as such a whimsical character that he seems to have stepped straight out of an operetta:

> Zelten had all those superb and conspicuous failings with which our countrymen had graced the Germans until 1870, failings with which they will soon have to endow another people if the Germans persist in wanting to be bold, rapacious, and practical; he had blond curly hair, he sacrificed every minute of his life to foolish fancies; he went down into pools fully dressed in order to put his hand on the fountain or to put the bill of the sleeping swan back under the right wing: he was Germany. (pp. 19–20)

Jean had known him at a boarding house in Munich seven years before the war. At that time Zelten had devised a system for settling the problem of Alsace-Lorraine with his French friend. He had made up two jigsaw puzzles, each of which was a map of the disputed territories cut out by districts. He gave him one, saying: "We must settle this business of the Reichsland . . . at least between the two of us. I have the same cut-out map. When I think that you are worthy of it, you or your country, I shall give you one district. You do the same. What a fine example we would give Europe if in six months you had my whole map and I had yours" (p. 25). Four years of war had not at all changed his spirit of generosity. On his left arm he bore the scar of a French bullet around which he had tattooed the following words: "The German to whom this skin belongs will never hate France" (p. 29). Yet the war taught him something else: ". . . we were separated by precisely those years when we were called upon to understand the world and its movement, and I doubt whether Newton, Archimedes, and Copernicus confided in their friends in the same way after their discoveries as before. It was not by seeing apples fall, but by seeing Germans fall (and I can see a poor fat one, bouncing!), that I became aware of the forces that were carrying me away and carrying Germany away" (pp. 31–32). Zelten's discovery is not spelled out in the novel; but as the story progresses and we become acquainted with Zelten's revolutionary objectives, it is evident that he fears the strength of German imperialism and would like to hold it in check by forming an alliance with France, which is the first point in his political platform (p. 247).

Even a character as whimsical and contradictory as Zelten is not purely fictitious. We may recall that Jean's acquaintance with Zelten dated from his student days in Munich before the war and that his first meeting with him after the war is in the Café de la Rotonde, frequented in 1916 by Trotsky, and a popular rendezvous for international spies, "defeatists," and Cubist painters. It is thus a fitting setting in which to introduce a tale of revolution and political intrigue. In a dispatch of Walter Duranty, Paris correspondent of the *New York Times,* recounting the Munich riots early in 1919,[12] we find the portrait of a striking model for Zelten, a man named Erich Mühsam, whom Duranty mentions as an example of prewar international anarchism. Duranty reports that Mühsam had lived in Paris in 1909 and was well known and sought after in the cafés of Montparnasse (of which the Café de la Rotonde was the most notorious). He was believed to have come from a very rich family, native of Munich, where he was received and respected by the elite of the city. This description fits Zelten perfectly, for the latter also had connections with the aristocracy and the *haute bourgeoisie* of Munich, and in Paris frequented the Montparnasse district, particularly the Café de la Rotonde. Ambroise Got also describes Mühsam in his book *La Terreur en Bavière,* where he classifies him as one of "the forces behind communism":

> A poet, an anarchist gentleman, who ends by becoming a people's commissar in the *Raeterepublik* of Bavaria, here we have one of the most astonishing cases luck would offer.
>
> Erich Mühsam, who was born in Berlin in 1878 and who likes to soar high in the clouds, far from earthly contingencies, calls himself amphigorically an "international revolutionary" and an "anarchist communist," the terms being interchangeable, acting as adjective or noun, as the reader wishes. . . .
>
> It would seem that he is not altogether responsible for his actions; he is fiery, muddle-headed, rash, and irresponsible. His political opinions do not appear to be solidly rooted. Although for years he has been professing anarchy, and according to his theory the State ought to be abolished, and although he says that Karl Marx was the biggest idiot in the history of the world, he is not afraid of associating with the most radical Communists in order

[12] February 15, 1919, 3:3.

to set up the least tolerable form of government: a dictatorship of the proletariat.

This modern Villon, with bright and twinkling eyes behind his pince-nez, a thick beard and a black mustache, a big shock of curly hair, looks more like a *chansonnier* from Montmartre than a formidable anarchist. Munich sovietism was the stumbling block of this Bohemian, who until then had been merely an inoffensive orator in bars and a lecturer in *café-chantants*. Cabaret footlights or the intimacy of the Weinstube, or "wine cellar," was more suitable to his talent than the glowing twilight of the Great Upheaval.[13]

The "black-banner aristocrat," as Got calls him, was certainly the most romantic personage of the Munich revolution and so akin to Giraudoux's hero, with his fiery nature, his contradictory political views, and his shock of curly hair, that he undoubtedly served as a model for Giraudoux's revolutionary. However, Zelten is probably, like Siegfried, a composite of several men who had struck Giraudoux's imagination. There were two other leftist leaders, Ernst Toller and Gustave Landauer, who also bear some resemblance to Zelten. Zelten, for example, had chosen his birthday to proclaim his dictatorship. We read in *La Terreur en Bavière* that Gustave Landauer had Bavaria proclaimed a Soviet Republic on April 7, his own birthday (p. 69). Furthermore, the very name of Zelten identifies him with the Communists, if one can attach any significance to the statement of Ambroise Got that the German Communist Party had its seat in Berlin *in den Zelten*.[14]

Were it not for these external sources, it would not be possible to identify the nature of Zelten's revolution with any degree of assurance. Giraudoux's mocking tone and offhand account do nothing to clarify Zelten's position. This is the way that Jean learns of Zelten's revolution:

[13] *La Terreur en Bavière* (Perrin et Cie, 1922), pp. 97–99.
[14] *L'Allemagne après la débâcle,* p. 67.

> One day, posted on the door of the Casino, I found a piece of news that drove us out of the Baltic.
>
> "Munich Revolution. Count Doctor Artist Painter von Zelten has assumed power."
>
> For, in Germany, it takes at least half the telegram to indicate the bourgeois titles of the revolutionary. (p. 233)

Zelten's movement appears here as a luxury item, a privilege of the nobility, the intellectuals, and the artists, there being no title associating it with the working class.

Zelten assumed power by means of a stratagem that is not found in Got's account, but in Homer. His assistant had put a hundred revolutionaries in the statue of Bavaria, where they had roasted the whole day; at eight o'clock they had charged the barracks and taken the Rathaus. There was only one death. "The spirit of the movement had not yet been very well determined, for in Schwabing they had arrested all the Jews, and in Haidhausen, three gatherings of seminarists, who were celebrating the nomination of a new nuncio. Actually, the second Bavarian Republic was already in discussion with the Vatican, and for the same reason as the first, its agents having requisitioned the nunciature's automobile because it was red in color" (p. 237). This amusing detail is borrowed from the journalists, for the same incident can be found in *La Terreur en Bavière* (p. 234).

Zelten seems as irresponsible in his political views as Erich Mühsam, which would explain up to a certain point the confusion about his revolution in the novel. "Zelten, from this information, seemed to me to be already compromising with his tastes and his hates, for what he detested most were electrical engineers and outdoor painters, and there was no mention of any of them having been hung or—a refinement that he had formerly set his mind on—electrocuted" (pp. 237-38). The reference to electrical engineers may be an allusion to André

Marty, chief engineer on board the destroyer *Protet* and insti-
gator of the first Black Sea rebellion; and Bohemian painters
were numerous among the revolutionaries in Bavaria. Therefore,
it would seem that Zelten was not, after all, the sworn enemy
of those who sympathized with the Russian Revolution. On the
contrary, according to the proclamation leaflets distributed by
airplane, the aim of his government was to fight Pan-Germanism
and "to distribute hectowatts equally on the head of every
Bavarian" (p. 239). This picturesque statement of the first point
in Lenin's program, the electrification of the country, is bound
to evoke a smile, but what is more important than the image
is the implication that Zelten is aiming at a kind of Soviet
revolution by promising to develop Bavaria's electric power for
the benefit of the entire population.

Another comic element which distracts the reader's attention
from the serious aims of Zelten's revolution is the introduction
of the mad Doctor Lipp, who, according to Giraudoux, was
"head of transportation for one hour in 1918 and had taken
advantage of it to declare war on Switzerland and Wurtemberg,
a war that he believed ever raging and that he was in haste to
bring to an end" (p. 247). This incredible character, who escaped from an insane asylum to join Zelten's revolution, was
actually a member of the Landauer government, serving as
Minister of Foreign Affairs in the *Raeterepublik*. Ambroise Got
gives the following account of Dr. Lipp's contribution to the
terror in Bavaria:

> Shortly after his nomination, seized by a fit of incredible and
> bellicose rage on hearing that a blockade was set up against So-
> viet Bavaria and that she was deprived of her means of transport,
> this hypocrite who talked of perpetual peace wrote his colleague
> Paulukum the following letter, which recalls the gestures of the
> heroes of farce:
> "My dear colleague, I have declared war on Wurtemberg and

Switzerland [*sic*], because those dogs did not want to lend us the 65 locomotives we had asked for. We are certain of victory. Moreover, I shall ask the Pope for his pontifical blessing."[15]

If the revolution of Zelten and his associates seems rather bizarre, it is no more so than the reality. In the case of Dr. Lipp, Giraudoux did not even bother to give him a fictitious name.

Another character, Lieviné Lieven, is a fusion of two historical figures. His name suggests the two Russians, Max Levien and Eugen Levine, whom Got lists among the "fanatics." When the Landauer government was overthrown by a counterrevolutionary *coup d'état,* which was, in turn, broken up by the Spartacus League, these men assumed power. They had formerly been associated with the moderate Communists, Mühsam, Toller, and Landauer, who at first supported them; but when the problem of supplies grew desperate and the white army threatened to attack Munich, the two factions finally fell out. The duumvirate Levien-Levine is the prototype of the character Lieviné Lieven, who shouts: "I have the two most beautiful names of the last revolution all to myself!" (p. 237). Zelten disapproves of Lieviné Lieven's movement (p. 245), which is quashed at the end of two weeks by a vote of the Assembly.

Zelten's brief revolution would fit equally well into the interval between the fall of the Levien-Levine dictatorship on April 27 and the arrival of the white troops on May 2, although Giraudoux dates the latter event June 3 (p. 247). But as we have seen, Giraudoux cannot be relied upon for dates, and he often telescopes several events and personages into one. In any case, we are dealing with the contrast not only between Zelten and Siegfried but also between Zelten and the "fanatics," who,

---

[15] *La Terreur en Bavière,* pp. 128–29. This episode is also recorded in more scholarly works. Cf. Harold J. Gordon, *The Reichswehr and the German Republic, 1919–1926* (Princeton: Princeton University Press, 1957), p. 44.

according to the novel, were foreigners and Semites, whereas Zelten would seem to represent a kind of purely indigenous and Aryan brand of communism. Lieviné Lieven accuses Zelten of wanting only Bavarians in Bavaria, and it is true that Zelten is one of those who believe in the existence of an international Jewish conspiracy, both in revolutionary circles and in high finance. he is against both Rathenau and Lieven because of their "Yiddish wailing." This absurdly contradictory point of view was widespread at the time, even among Social Democrats and Independents, and it would seem that Giraudoux shared it.

Zelten's revolution fails, thanks to the intervention of American and British financiers, who are in control of German affairs behind the façade of the parliamentary democracy represented by Siegfried. When Siegfried comes on behalf of Parliament to ask for Zelten's abdication, the latter makes no mistake about the true nature of the opposition:

> "Gentlemen," said Zelten, "in one hour I will have left the palace. It is not you who are driving me out, nor is it Germany. I continue to believe that all true Germans are in favor of peace, love of the arts, and fraternity. What has expelled me are two telegrams to Berlin, which have been intercepted. Here they are: the first comes from America and is addressed to Wirth. It reads: 'If Zelten remains Munich, will cancel oil contract.' The second comes from London and is addressed to Stinnes: 'If Zelten remains Munich, will cancel Volga contract and cause rise in mark.'" (p. 269)

At the end of his speech Zelten accuses Siegfried of being an element foreign to Germany. It is a pity that the author does not give Siegfried the opportunity to answer his rival. It is, therefore, up to the reader to draw his own conclusions. Zelten's government would have exploited the treasures of Germany for the benefit of the German people, while at the same time seeking an alliance with France; Siegfried's government sought to protect the rights of German and foreign capitalists with the support of the Allied powers. Zelten complains bitterly about the splendid opportunity which has been missed:

> The unfortunate thing is that I have the nation with me and that I am forsaking it. Do not believe that opium, cocaine, and morphine addicts were the only active agents of my uprising. But the great peoples, except perhaps for France, like to be governed and ruled only by those who do not share their concerns. The moment the god of poetry and romanticism stirs up sixty million men, as is true in Germany at this time, they give themselves body and soul to oil traffickers. (p. 265)

The role of oil in European affairs is pointed out elsewhere by Jean de Pierrefeu in his account of the Geneva Conference, which Giraudoux mentions at the beginning of the novel:

> The chorus of the occult delegates of trade, which was the counterpart of the majestic chorus of diplomats and politicians, played its part without stop during the five weeks of the conference. Around us we heard disturbing sirens modulate the cantilène of raw materials, the ballad of exportation, and above all, the hymn to oil, full-volumed and religious, like church music. Reportedly, this hymn to nutritive and fruitful oil, more precious than gold, and which all the great nations are fighting to possess, caught the ear of Lloyd George himself, who willingly listened.[16]

Twenty years later when he wrote *La Folle de Chaillot,* Giraudoux was to take his revenge on the "oil traffickers," whom he blamed for starting wars and quashing popular revolutions.

What, then, is the relationship between Siegfried and the Limousin—between Germany and its sister Republic? Zelten speaks jokingly of his surprise when he first noted in France "the reign of the small land-owner, which leaves American bankers speechless at the windows of the Cherbourg express"

---

[16] *La Saison diplomatique* (Paris: Aubier, 1926), p. 224.

(p. 32) and which blinds the French to the expansionist temperament of their neighbor beyond the Rhine. Later, in his program note to *Siegfried,* Giraudoux was to warn against the trusting ignorance of his nation:

> A Frenchman cannot afford to be the slightest bit wrong in his relations with Germany, even on the count of not knowing her. When one lives near a country that is perpetually impelled to a paroxysm of activity, to delusions of grandeur, to a brutal love of the whole world, that country must, above all, never feel that near her, ignorant and without curiosity, is the neighbor to whom fate has welded her.

This is essentially what Zelten is trying to tell Jean in their first meeting in the Café de la Rotonde. The failure of both Zelten and Siegfried to curb the extremist passions of their countrymen and channel them into a democratic and pacifistic form of government bodes ill for the future.

If the meaning of the novel is not clear on a first reading, it is not surprising. Giraudoux has that most engaging failing of the French, an irrepressible drollery and a mania for playing with ideas, especially those about which he feels most deeply. His irreverent treatment of serious subjects is a sort of modesty which conceals profound and coherent thought. Moreover, Giraudoux had no intention of sacrificing his literary style to polemic. On the contrary, one might say that he wrote *Siegfried et le Limousin* as if some wager were involved to show that a journalistic account can be transformed into a work of symbolist fiction. This stylistic exercise may have been a catharsis for the pamphlets he did not deign or dare to write. At any rate, it was a useful experience which served him well when he brought his novel to the stage.

✧ III ✧

Siegfried von Kleist

The genesis of a creative work is often what is least known about it, and what the critic is most curious to discover. In the case of the play *Siegfried,* it is possible to satisfy one's curiosity more easily than usual. We know that this work had its origins in the novel,[1] and it is not difficult to determine why Giraudoux wanted to bring *Siegfried et le Limousin* to the stage rather than *Suzanne et le Pacifique* or *Juliette au pays des hommes.* The first had the advantage of being a prize-winning novel dealing with a subject of current interest which would be more likely to appeal to the theatre-going public than the interior

---

[1] This is not the opinion of the French critic, R. M. Albérès, in his complementary thesis *La Genèse de Siegfried,* 1963. He sees in the novel nothing more than what Giraudoux called a poetic divagation, and he denies that it contributed any more to the play than the setting and the cast of characters. He sees no political significance at all in the novel and very little in the play, which he treats primarily as an example of a well-constructed drama. In order to make his debut in the theatre with *Siegfried,* Giraudoux forced himself to subordinate his poetic imagination to the rigorous discipline of playwriting with the diligent application of the good student translating from French into Latin, Albérès contends. This is the point which he elaborates in 150 pages of well-documented text. He makes no attempt to show the evolution of the author's political message, having denied that the novel contains one. He takes Giraudoux's anti-realism very seriously and prefers to treat his works in a cosmic context. Giraudoux's only theme, according to Albérès, is the confrontation of men and gods, although the author admits that this has no place in *Siegfried.*

monologues of *Suzanne* and *Juliette*. It was perhaps the success
of the novel that led some of Giraudoux's friends and admirers
to urge him to try playwriting, in particular the father of his
young friend Paul Morand. "If I wrote for the theatre, it was
thanks to your father," Giraudoux used to say to him.[2] Morand's
father had advised the novelist to draw on his own books if he
did not know where to begin. According to another witness, it
was the critic Benjamin Crémieux who urged Giraudoux to
make a play of *Siegfried et le Limousin*.[3] Giraudoux took the
advice of both men, but the reason which he later gave is significant: "I thought theatre might offer me a means of expression
that was more likely to reach the general public directly. Even
in the novel I wanted to reach that goal. The critics did not
seem to understand my idea, and I persisted in trying to put it
across. Theatre appeared to me the most suitable vehicle for the
purpose. There the characters are shown in relief and convey
the idea directly and more inevitably."[4] While it is not always
safe to take Giraudoux at his word in these newspaper interviews, the great number of fragments which he published on
the Siegfried theme is evidence of the importance he attached
to communicating his views on the Franco-German problem.

Even so, chance played an important part in the genesis of
Siegfried. On the occasion of the retirement of Charles Andler,
Giraudoux's professor of German at the École Normale, some
of his friends and students prepared a *Festschrift*[5] in his honor,
and Giraudoux was among those asked to contribute an article.
On the surface, nothing could have been more natural than to
present the master with a dramatic adaptation of a scene from

[2] Paul Morand, *Souvenirs de notre jeunesse*, p. 143.

[3] Jean Barreyre in *Candide*, March 24, 1928.

[4] *L'Intransigeant*, August 9, 1928.

[5] *Mélanges offerts à M. Charles Andler par ses amis et élèves* (Strasbourg, 1924).

his novel *Siegfried et le Limousin*. After all, as an authority on Pan-Germanism,[6] Andler may well have inspired the author's main thesis. But whatever Giraudoux owed to Charles Andler he was tardy in acknowledging, if we are to accept the word of a former classmate,[7] who informs us that relations between Giraudoux and Andler were cordial but short-lived; the former had not even sent the specialist on Germany a copy of his novel, whereas he did send Barrès a copy of *Suzanne et le Pacifique*. Since Giraudoux had never passed the *agrégation* in German, one is tempted to believe that relations between the two were in fact less than cordial, especially on the part of Giraudoux. In any case, his contribution to the *Mélanges offerts à M. Charles Andler* is a very curious homage, not to say an impertinent one.

One can imagine the impression these first lines must have made sandwiched between an article by André Fauconnet on the teaching of phonetics and a comparative study by A. Jolivet of Gerhard Hauptmann's *The Winter Ballad* and Selma Lagerlöf's *Herr Arnes Pennigar:*

> GENEVIÈVE: Where are we?
>
> ROBINEAU: My captain, who used to sleep on his horse during marches, also would awake and call out to me: Where are we? I would answer him with the number of kilometers: we had gone 20, we had gone 40. Today we have gone 845 kilometers. . . . Guess.
>
> GENEVIÈVE: It's an egg.[8]

---

[6] Charles Andler, *Le Pangermanisme, ses plans d'expansion allemande dans le monde* (Paris: Colin, 1915).

[7] Jean-Marc Aucuy, *La Jeunesse de Giraudoux*.

[8] This answer was doubtless inspired by an episode in *Siegfried et le Limousin* (p. 70): "I have not lost the hope of some day finding the answer, in Oceania or in Mexico, to a few other riddles of my past: a knot always ends by coming undone, merely out of disgust at being a knot. As a matter of fact, the only one that's really on my mind is the Tornielli riddle; that ambassador in office, whom I saw for the first time when prizes were being awarded for the national lycée competition, ges-

ROBINEAU: What?

GENEVIÈVE: Do excuse me. But every time someone asks me to guess a riddle, I have got into the habit, since childhood, of answering: It's an egg. That's the answer which has been most successful. . . . Why have you carried me off, do you love me?

ROBINEAU: No.

GENEVIÈVE: But are we going to live together?

ROBINEAU: Why not?[9]

What are these trivia doing amidst such learned studies? In this bit of dialogue the character Robineau has replaced Jean, the narrator of the novel, that is to say Jean Giraudoux himself, who in honor of his former professor has assumed the title of *agrégé des lettres,* which the University had not conferred on him. Moreover, the degree seems to be a fixed idea with him, for in those five pages the word *agrégé* appears four times, with other more or less comic references to the University. Robineau, for instance, evokes for his traveling companion a vision of Germany in which the uninitiated discerns merely the poet's originality, but in which Andler's students would recognize the three great periods in the literary history of the country listed in the programs for the *agrégation:*[10] "the night was well-ordered and drawn like one of Albrecht Dürer's nights. . . . We were in that epic time of the Holy Empire, which still survived in Germany during the morning, whereas the romantic period never became apparent until around noon, and at twilight, that of the *Sturm*

---

tured to me to come over to him, and into my hand he slipped a hard-boiled egg." Tornielli's egg has become a legend in the University. I heard this anecdote related by M. Paul Etard, librarian at the École Normale.

[9] *Mélanges,* p. 156.

[10] For the programs that Giraudoux prepared for the *agrégation,* see Laurent Le Sage's article, "Giraudoux's German Studies," *Modern Language Quarterly,* XII, No. 3 (September 1951), 353–59.

und Drang."[11] Here the mockery is veiled, but it is undeniable when Geneviève says to Robineau: "I hope that you snore, too; they snore in the University." This is the next-to-the-last sentence of Giraudoux's contribution to the *Mélanges offerts à M. Charles Andler.*

Giraudoux had his little revenge, no doubt of it. The fact becomes more apparent when we realize that the first draft of that scene is derived not from the novel but from a short piece entitled "Vacances sur un chagrin,"[12] which came out four years before *Siegfried et le Limousin* and has the same narrator as that of his autobiographical novel *Simon le Pathétique* (1918). What is the hero's *chagrin*—a disappointment in love, or his failure to pass the examination for the *agrégation?* We don't know. "And so began the holidays. There was a gulf between me and my life . . . ," writes Simon. To console himself, he jumps on a train headed for the Bosphorus, determined to stay on until he has to change cars. Next day, as the express is pulling out of Munich, Simon sees the shapes, one after another, of the Munich monuments whose names Giraudoux made such fun of in his novel: the Glyptotek, the Pinakoteks, Bavaria, whose head could comfortably hold twelve women (in the novel it houses one hundred revolutionaries),[13] and the Maximilianeum. Suddenly the narrative is broken by a brief scene. "It was then that Lyzica came out of her compartment" (Lyzica is a Roumanian girl who helped him forget for two days):

"We are in Munich," I explained to her.
"Ah!" she said.

Who would have predicted that ten years later this minimal dialogue would evolve into the eloquent lines of *Siegfried?* The

---

[11] *Mélanges,* p. 159. Cf. *Siegfried et le Limousin,* p. 63.
[12] *Les Ecrits Nouveaux,* II (1918), 265–72.
[13] *Siegfried et le Limousin,* p. 238. See above, p. 52.

resemblance between the 1918 fragment and the homage to Andler is slight, but in the former one perceives the nucleus of the latter: the arrival in Munich with a traveling companion (called Lyzica, not Geneviève, although the name Geneviève does appear elsewhere in the "Vacances"), and the jokes about the Munich monuments. The humor is a little forced, however, and the general tone of the piece is somber in contrast to the farcical scene of the *Mélanges,* whose primary objective seems to have been to poke fun at the academic world and especially at Charles Andler.

Actually, the novel itself is a very subtle spoof of Andler's manner and ideas. To Giraudoux's fellow students, his pages on Pan-Germanism must have suggested an unfavorable comparison between the ponderous style of the scholar and the agile wit of the novelist. If these students had deciphered the political message of the novel, which cautions the French against the camouflage of parliamentary democracy in Germany, they would have noted some important differences between the viewpoints of the two men. Charles Andler had treated the problem of Germany in an important work entitled *La Décomposition politique du socialisme allemand 1914–1919,*[14] of which the underlying philosophy is the decay of Marxism. Whereas Andler saw in the failure of the revolutionary upsurge in Germany the proof of what he had been saying for ten years, namely, that Marxism was an obsolete doctrine, Giraudoux more realistically ascribed it to the secret intervention of American and British financiers. Moreover, Andler considered the German Communists to be the sworn enemies of the Entente, while Giraudoux depicted them, in the character of Zelten, as the only true friends of France. In writing the novel Giraudoux did in his witty and nonchalant way try to rebut some of Andler's teachings, perhaps out of spite but above all because he felt that his position in the diplomatic

[14] Paris: Bossard, 1919.

service and his artistic intuition qualified him to speak with more authority on the subject than this eminent scholar.

The five-page sally which Giraudoux published in honor of Charles Andler certainly does not betray any serious vein of political thought nor any ambition to become a dramatist, but the idea of a dramatic presentation of his novel had been planted, and was to germinate as circumstances provided a new stimulus. A brief assignment in Berlin from May to October 1924 gave Giraudoux an opportunity to observe the workings of the German Republic at first hand.[15] His subsequent appointment as head of the press and information service kept him in the mainstream of foreign affairs but left him little time to write. In April 1926 he first made the acquaintance of Louis Jouvet, the celebrated actor and director,[16] and this provided the spur he needed to embark on the career of a playwright. Toward the end of 1926 Giraudoux was retired from the Office of the Press to a more peaceful corner of the Ministry, where he found the leisure to produce for the theatre. Meanwhile, events on the international front made the subject which he embodied in his character Siegfried even more relevant. On October 16, 1925 the Treaty of Locarno was signed, which prepared the way for the admission of Germany to the League of Nations on September 8, 1926. On the surface everything announced a new era of peace and prosperity, but Giraudoux, from his observation post at the Quai d'Orsay, was still pessimistic. Marshal von Hindenburg had become President of the Reich in 1925, and that same year Hitler published *Mein Kampf*. In short, the wave of militarism and extremism seemed to be rising, and the confidence which the Allies were placing in the renascent Germany seemed to some

[15] See Appendix I, Giraudoux's chronology furnished by the Ministry of Foreign Affairs.
[16] Maurice Bourdet, "La Genèse de Siegfriend," *Nouvelles Littéraires,* May 19, 1928.

observers unjustified and even dangerous. Giraudoux was among these, as an analysis of the first version of his *Siegfried* will show.

Sometime during 1927 Giraudoux produced the first complete dramatic adaptation of *Siegfried et le Limousin*. This has been published by Ides et Calendes in the first volume of the *Variantes* under the title *Siegfried von Kleist,* and it differs substantially from the *Siegfried* staged by Louis Jouvet on May 3, 1928 at the Champs-Elysées Theatre. The *Siegfried von Kleist* is particularly significant because it contains by far the clearest exposition of the author's ideas on Franco-German relations. These ideas were obscured in the novel by the mass of extraneous material, and they are modified considerably in the final version of the play to conform to the optimism then current. The original version, therefore, provides an important key to those works as well as an interesting study in the making of a dramatist.

Giraudoux may not have exaggerated when he declared in an interview with Frédéric Lefèvre, and precisely apropos of *Siegfried et le Limousin:* "I take a clean page and I begin to write; the characters originate as I go along; at the end of five or six pages, I see where I'm headed. . . ."[17] This method of composing does no particular damage to his novels, where form is less important than style; but in the theatre, where unity of action is indispensable, it is easy to see why Giraudoux preferrerd to work with a familiar plot rather than to invent a new one. In adapting his novel to the stage, he rearranged a number of details in order to achieve a more tightly knit plot and to focus attention on the political theme. The date of the dramatic action remains the same. Directly following the cast of characters, he gives the time of the play as early January 1922, but in the opening scene he refers to the place "where Eisner fell, assassinated, one month ago" (p. 14). This reference immediately sets the tone of the play and prepares for the melodramatic dénouement. But to any-

---

[17] *Une Heure avec . . .* (1st Ser.), p. 149.

one who happened to recall that Eisner died on February 22, 1919, it is as confusing as the chronology established on the first page of the novel. This inconsistency would hardly have gone unnoticed if Giraudoux had not corrected it in the final version.

The setting of *Siegfried von Kleist* is confined to Germany, thus eliminating the picturesque introductory scene between Jean and Zelten at the Café de la Rotonde. This meeting place of painters, spies, and revolutionaries would have made a much more colorful backdrop than a boarding house in Munich, which is the scene of the first act. But if Giraudoux did not manage to use all the rich material of the novel in his first play, he was to draw on it for his last. The sidewalk of the Café Francis in the first act of *La Folle de Chaillot* recalls in many ways the scene at the Café de la Rotonde in *Siegfried et le Limousin*.

Giraudoux creates several new characters for the play. He replaces the narrator Jean by the Robineau of the scene he wrote for Andler, which serves as his point of departure for the first version. But the Robineau of *Siegfried von Kleist* is not quite so easily identified with Jean as the Robineau of the *Mélanges*. In fact, in some respects he appears to be a caricature of Andler himself. He now has his degree in grammar and philology, not in letters, and his views on the importance of philology recall those of Charles Andler. So do the following lines: "The Revolution, Geneviève? You can set your mind at rest. I have only to appear in a city or an epoch for any event of historical importance to fade away. History fights shy of me as if I were an *agrégé* in history and not a grammarian" (p. 14). Since Charles Andler had written a volume on the decline of Marxism without deigning to mention the Russian Revolution, this rather puzzling complaint of Robineau's would seem to be an ironic allusion to the scholar's obtuse political views. There is also an incident in the second act which is difficult to explain unless one identifies Robineau with Andler.

For the first stage adaptation, Giraudoux created an entirely new character, Muck, a spy who is in league with Zelten. Muck is the most eccentric and inoffensive of informers, half *littérateur* and half clown, like Zelten himself. His role seems to have been created to counterbalance that of Eva, who is also introduced as a spy. From the very first, Eva is portrayed as the embodiment of the political power which is using Siegfried and which is unalterably opposed to Zelten, while her role as Siegfried's nurse and tutor is considerably reduced. In the second act Giraudoux highlights the political conflict by creating the roles of three Prussian generals— Waldorf, Ledinger, and Fontgeloy—who are the most bitter enemies of France. General Fontgeloy originally appeared in a fragment entitled *"Visite chez le Prince,"* which Giraudoux published in 1923. He is a spiritual descendant of those French Protestant emigrants of the seventeenth and eighteenth centuries who became more Prussian than the Prussians; and he represents the extremist groups who are plotting a war of revenge against the French as soon as possible. Giraudoux has Fontgeloy introduce himself as another Forestier or Siegfried, implying that if this twentieth-century French emigrant remains in Germany, he, too, will become a dangerous foe of the Allies. The other names in the cast of characters are familiar to the readers of the novel, although their roles are slightly changed.

One of Giraudoux's favorite lines is "Destiny's personnel obeys without a summons." And so it does in the novel. For the most part, the characters appear and disappear, speak or keep silent without any apparent reason other than the author's whim. But in adapting his loosely knit plot for the stage, Giraudoux made a conscious effort to provide a logical motivation for his characters. The arrival of Robineau and Geneviève in Munich is explained in the opening scene as the result of a telegram from Zelten, beseeching them to come immediately for a mysterious reason having to do with the fate of France and Germany. Thus the political nature of their mission is established from the outset, although the details are not spelled out until the sixth scene, when Robineau is finally face to face with Zelten. Here again a number of important modifications follow. It is Zelten and not Jean whose suspicions have been aroused by Siegfried's articles in the *Frankfurter Zeitung*. Zelten informs Robineau that he suspects his political opponent Siegfried of being the French journalist Jacques Forestier, who is supposed to have been killed at the beginning of the war. Zelten wants Robineau and Geneviève to unmask this impostor and prevent him from becoming President of the German Republic. The role of Geneviève becomes much more significant than in the novel. She is introduced as Forestier's fiancée instead of Zelten's ex-wife, and she takes over Jean's role of French tutor and companion to Siegfried. She and Eva now have contrasting roles as images of Siegfried's two mother countries, and they are both directly involved in the political intrigues surrounding him.

These intrigues are exposed in the second and third scenes where Siegfried's doorkeeper, Muck, is preparing to receive, in the same boarding house where Robineau and Geneviève are staying, the parents of soldiers who were reported missing during the war. They hope to find their lost son in the person of Siegfried, who arrives in the fourth scene. It soon becomes apparent that Zelten is behind this effort to pierce the mystery of Siegfried's lost identity and that Muck is his spy. In the third scene Muck and Zelten discover that they in turn are being spied upon by Eva, who is eavesdropping behind a door which Muck opens. She accuses Zelten of plotting against Siegfried and against sixty million Germans. Zelten points out that they are defending different causes: Siegfried is dedicated to adopting a constitution for Germany, which Zelten declares is as whimsical as trying to make Siegfried's dragon swallow an alarm clock in order to teach him to tell time (p. 31). This amusing analogy,

which also appears in the novel, is as prophetic as it is picturesque. Eva mocks Zelten, saying that his supporters are mostly
opium and morphine addicts. Zelten retorts that Siegfried is
backed by Marshal von Hindenburg and General von Ludendorff, whereas he has on his side the whole army of dead poets
and musicians. Zelten is pitting the temperament of an eighteenth-
century romantic against that of a twentieth-century milita-
rist. His positive political program is not revealed until the
second act, but he is portrayed by Robineau in the introductory
scene as the embodiment of everything that is admirable and
generous in the German people. "Ah! How simplified Franco-
German relations would have been with Germans like him!"
Robineau exclaims (pp. 17–18).

Siegfried makes a brief entrance in the fourth scene to allow
the parents an opportunity to identify him as a lost son, but in
vain. Eva consoles him with the words: "Don't despair. One day
all this darkness will open wide its gates and your mother will
be announced" (p. 43). At that moment the door opens and Muck
announces Marshal von Hindenburg and General von Ludendorff. "Illustrious mothers, too illustrious . . . show them in," replies Siegfried. Siegfried is thus identified from the very beginning with the German Republic born of the armistice.[18] The
symbol is transparent, too transparent no doubt, since Giraudoux
eliminated the scene in the final version. He did, however, value
it highly enough to publish it in 1930 with some other variants
under the title *"Fugues sur Siegfried."*

The mystery of Siegfried's lost identity is revealed in the subsequent scenes between Zelten, Robineau, and Geneviève. By
linking Geneviève with Siegfried's past instead of with Zelten's,
Giraudoux has introduced a love interest that was lacking in the

[18] Marshal von Hindenburg became President of the German Republic
in 1925.

novel. The first act reaches a one-sided emotional climax when Geneviève finally comes face to face with Siegfried and recognizes him as her lost lover Forestier. But there is no answering flicker of recognition on the part of the German statesman, who remains impassive and somewhat puzzled by the emotionally charged silence of Geneviève. At the recommendation of Robineau, who acts as her spokesman, Siegfried hesitantly engages her to give him French lessons.

The second act of *Siegfried von Kleist* takes place in Siegfried's office, where Professor Schmeck and General Fontgeloy are ransacking the drawers of Siegfried's desk at the behest of Eva, who is alarmed by the discovery of Zelten's conspiracy. In the novel Professor Schmeck had a shadowy role as the head of a hospital for amnesia victims in which Siegfried was interned. Schmeck was also the president of several hate societies and had important connections with the great German industralists. However, it is not clear in what capacity he bore the title of professor. In the play Giraudoux clarifies this point in an unexpected way by making him a philologist. This leads to an amusing scene between Schmeck and Robineau in which their political hostility suddenly dissolves when they discover that they have the same specialty. Schmeck's role in the play is primarily that of spokesman for the supporters of Siegfried:

> I did not give him the education of a dauphin in Germany, I did not have the bed in which that three-year-old German adult was wailing surrounded, in turn, by wet nurses who were named Rathenau or Erzberger, and good fairies called Stresemann or Krupp, in order to restore to him, at precisely the moment that Germany would use him, the brain of a French *petit bourgeois*. . . . You see this fatal equilibrium in which we are struggling. Fate is trying to deprive our country of a clear view of its destiny, by dividing it into two equal parts, two absolutely equal parts: thirty million on the right, thirty million on the left. Siegfried

alone will be able to tilt the balance from one side to the other by his own weight. (p. 66)

This statement of the political mission of Siegfried is seconded by General Fontgeloy, representing an association of Prussian army officers who are plotting a war of revenge against France. In the play it is this newly created character[19] who issues the warning—this time to Geneviève instead of to Jean—that she and Robineau will be expelled from Germany if they attempt to interfere with Siegfried's political career. Furthermore, Fontgeloy warns that Siegfried will not be permitted to leave the country alive. These threats are interrupted by the cannon shot announcing Zelten's revolution. Fontgeloy's first reaction betrays his innermost thought, which is shared by two other generals, Waldorf and Ledinger, to whom Giraudoux gives minor roles in the play:

WALDORF: Well! Fontgeloy, you have heard the news?
FONTGELOY: Yes, war. War with France?
WALDORF: Your're behind the times, Fontgeloy.
LEDINGER: You're ahead of time, Fontgeloy. (p. 91)

In the sinister words of Ledinger, "You're ahead of time, Fontgeloy," there is a hint of the militarists' designs against France. It is a less direct way of depicting the German spirit of revenge than the racist teachings of Eva in the novel,[20] which would have seemed too extravagant in this new era of optimism. The ensuing discussion between the generals centers on a definition of war, inspired no doubt by the debates in the League of Nations. The cynical formulas expounded by Waldorf and Ledinger have a familiar ring even today: war is the nation; war is the League of Nations; war is peace (pp. 93–94).

Although the introduction of Professor Schmeck and the gen-

[19] See p. 67
[20] See p. 47.

erals clarifies the political role cut out for Siegfried, we never hear the statesman's own political views. Siegfried is portrayed primarily as a straw man, whose every attribute has been carefully selected and nurtured by his adoptive countrymen. He seems to have no will or power of his own. He is simply the symbol of constitutional government, by which a coalition of forces, including the German militarists, hopes to unite this sharply divided people and to keep them from going over to the Soviet camp.

With the announcement that Zelten has taken power, the nature of his political opposition is elaborated, but only indirectly. The generals hear the report of his *coup d'état,* but we don't see the revolutionaries at work until Act III. As in the novel, the aim of Zelten's revolution is to combat Pan-Germanism and to distribute equally the treasures of Bavarian electrical power (p. 92). But this program is not enough to identify him definitely with the Bolsheviks. His name, Count von Zelten, confuses the issue.[21] According to one of the generals, "the bourgeois don't dare take sides, for they don't know, because of Zelten's name, whether he is instigating a royalist or a soviet revolution, and they read his proclamation with sympathy, if anything" (p. 92).[22]

Zelten is as much aware of the sharp division of political opinion within Germany as Siegfried's supporters are, but he is trying to unite the country in a different way and for a different purpose. He has a tangible program that could conceivably lead to peace and prosperity, but he has no form of government to

[21] See pp. 51–52.

[22] Giraudoux's love of paradox and ambiguity seems to have been a not uncommon trait in his generation. Zelten's politics are no more paradoxical than those of his prototype, Erich Mühsam. André du Fresnoy is another case in point. This journalist, whose untimely death may have inspired the creation of the Siegfried myth, was also known for his contradictory political views. His ability to work successfully for newspapers of opposing political parties obviously impressed Giraudoux, who endowed Jacques Forestier with the same quality. See p. 41

propose. Siegfried, on the other hand, has a constitution but no specific program. However, he has the support of the most powerful groups in the country, whereas Zelten's partisans, in addition to the drug addicts, include the staffs of the swimming pools and theatres! "Theatres, swimming pools, everything that's turbulent at times of merrymaking is turbulent today, and it makes the city seem like a carnival" (p. 92). Though Zelten has little opposition from the petty bourgeois, the power is so clearly on Siegfried's side that Zelten's coup is but an empty gesture and its outcome a foregone conclusion.

The carnival is still in progress in the opening scenes of the third act, which take place in the throne room of the Residency of the Wittelsbachs. Muck is having a telephone installed, and Zelten is trying out the throne. What first impresses him from his lofty perch is the prominent position of his legs. As he reflects on his illustrious predecessors, he suddenly realizes why so many of them were identified by their extremities: Bertha of the Big Foot, Charles the Knock-kneed, Otto the Clubfooted. In the midst of this jocular dialogue, Robineau arrives to offer congratulations. The badinage continues as Zelten nonchalantly informs him that he has arrived just in time for the abdication. However, he hints darkly that it will soon be Siegfried's turn.

Zelten is not quite the tyrant that some feared. He is willing to submit to the will of Parliament and is awaiting its decision, which Siegfried is to bring him. But he has no illusions as to the outcome. He knows that the members of Parliament are against him, especially Siegfried, whom he has consistently opposed. In spite of Zelten's title of nobility and his aspiration to the throne of the Wittelsbachs, he is clearly not a royalist. On the other hand, though his surname and the nature of his political program identify him with the Communists, Zelten is opposed to the brand of international Communism represented by Russian Jews such as Max Levien and Eugen Levine, the extremists of the Munich revolutionary movement.[23] Giraudoux makes this point in a rather disagreeable scene, which varies in a puzzling way from the details of the novel. During Zelten's brief reign, while waiting for Parliament to adjourn, he condemns to death an old Galician Jew, Liévine Liéven, who is accused of having disfigured and killed one of Zelten's friends. Despite a slight change in accent marks, the name is familiar to the readers of the novel, although the character is almost unrecognizable. He is now portrayed as a bandit, who has burned off the lines on his palms and fingers to avoid detection. Curiously enough, André Beucler in *Les Instants de Giraudoux* infers from this incident that Giraudoux was evoking the future Hitler (p. 143); but as I have already shown, Liévine Liéven can be more readily identified with the duumvirate Eugen Levine and Max Levien—emulators of Lenin, according to Ambroise Got—who "tyrannized" Munich from April 13 to 27.[24] In the novel Giraudoux had treated this revolutionary much more lightly. The detail of the undecipherable palms was explained as a childhood accident resulting from contact with a corrosive. This detail serves in turn to explain why the Liévine Lieven of the novel was so obsessed with the desire to read other people's palms, not being able to read his own! Zelten's friend, Lerchenfeld, whom the Liévine Liéven of the play is supposed to have tortured and killed, was Zelten's adversary in *Siegfried et le Limousin,* having gathered his troops at Dachau to bring about Zelten's downfall. All these confusing and seemingly pointless changes may be intended to distinguish moderate revolutionaries such as Zelten from terrorists and fanatics such as Liéven. The latter was portrayed in the novel as the leader of a rival revolutionary movement, which had been supplanted by Zelten's. Zelten disapproved of Lieven's revolution because it was led by

[23] See page 54.
[24] *La Terreur en Bavière,* p. 171.

Russian Jews, but there was no hint that Lieven was a criminal or a terrorist. He was just another of the mad revolutionaries. It is therefore surprising to see Zelten judge him so severely in the dramatic adaptation.

That scene is troubling in another respect as well. Robineau, who is present at the condemnation, begs Zelten to pardon the prisoner because he is the sole survivor of the vanished town of Slop, the region in which Yiddish originated. The philologian seems to be hypnotized by the vocables the prisoner pronounces but is completely indifferent to the crimes he is supposed to have committed. This emphasis on words and this indifference to acts may be another touch of satire directed against the obtuseness of Charles Andler. In any case, the little scene has a distinctly unpleasant flavor, combining political bad faith, anti-Semitism, and a cruel caricature of the philologian.

Fortunately, it is not part of the final version of the play, but it was published in July 1928, three months after the first performance, in *La Nouvelle Revue Française* under the title "Divertissement sur Siegfried." The "Divertissement" includes all the comic scenes in the Wittelsbach palace, which were eliminated in the final version, *Siegfried*. This cut, while eliminating a great deal of confusion and buffoonery, reduced the role of Zelten to the point where the nature of his revolution in the final version is open to all kinds of conjecture. It was, perhaps, to cover himself from the possible interpretation that he was defending a Bolshevist uprising in Germany—as he did in the novel—that Giraudoux decided to make this fragment public. At that time, the perceptive reader of the "Divertissement" would have been reassured that Zelten was a known enemy of the Bolsheviks and that only a university professor would have been naive enough to pardon an individual like Liévine Liéven. Decidedly, the diplomat has taken over here as in many other instances relating to the composition of the final version.

The scene of the condemnation is only the beginning of a long and involved preparation for the confrontation of Zelten and Siegfried and the unmasking of the latter. Zelten's downfall is presented with the same profusion of detail as in the novel. After the requisition of the nunciature's red automobile, after the profession of loyalty offered by the holy tribe of Oberammergau, whose spokesman is called Judas, Zelten receives the Mandatory of the Senate and the House, Siegfried von Kleist. Siegfried is escorted by troops, who surround the palace. He therefore comes in the name of the civil and military power to expel Zelten. But before stepping down, Zelten exposes two important secrets of the opposition: the intervention of foreign capital and the fact that Siegfried is an impostor. As in the novel, he has intercepted two telegrams, one from London and the other from Morgan and Rockefeller. "These are the two threats which correspond to the excommunication of the old days," he says. "I have made the last effort to keep Germany from becoming a combine, and I have failed. So may our Rhine, which was rough for a moment, be calmed by mineral oil . . . I am leaving . . . " (p. 123). Zelten exits by the back stairs but not before accusing Siegfried of imposture and Eva and Schmeck of complicity in the deception.

One would have expected this dramatic scene to be a fitting climax to the third act, but Giraudoux caps the political climax with an emotional one by liquidating the theme of Siegfried's lost identity. Siegfried, alone with Eva, demands an explanation. He now recalls with horror the procession of foreign prisoners he had passed in the courtyard and whom his soldiers had orders to shoot. This poignant reminder of his possible fate does not appear in the novel. When Eva, who has been sworn to secrecy, refuses to reveal his real identity, he has her read aloud the foreign news in the hope of recognizing his true country, his true race. This device is adapted very effectively from the novel.

Eva's hesitation before the ridiculous fact that freight cars loaded with elephants have collided in the station at Brive suggests to Siegfried that he is of French extraction. From the reader's point of view, what is revealing in this absurd news item is the innocence of France, who in the daily catastrophes of this world can lay claim only to that grotesque collision. And how typical of Giraudoux to characterize France in this way.

Pressed again by Siegfried, Eva finally corroborates his suspicions and reveals that he is the Frenchman, Jacques Forestier. Siegfried is then faced with his former fiancée, Geneviève Prat. The long-awaited scene of recognition, which is missing in the novel, does not fully materialize here either. Siegfried has recovered his name but not his memory, so that the awkward attempts of Geneviève to recall the life they once shared arouse no response on the part of the amnesic lover. Siegfried remains wooden to the end, and Act III is mercifully terminated by the news that Zelten has crossed the border by plane and that the crowd is waiting to acclaim Siegfried. The sentimental theme is thus conveniently disposed of, and the way is prepared for a purely political dénouement.

Despite the wealth of material and the somewhat bewildering mixture of farce, satire, melodrama, and pathos, there is a remarkable unity of action in the composition of Act III. It is even a masterpiece of clarity as compared with the confused and illogical sequence of events in the novel. *Siegfried et le Limousin* included such *hors d'oeuvres* as the description of Molière's anniversary celebration and an enigmatic exchange of letters between Jean and Lieviné Lieven's mistress during their brief imprisonment. Furthermore, the six-page account of Geneviève's death seemed pointless when her life had contributed so little to the dramatic action of the novel. And the political consequences of Zelten's disclosures were related only indirectly in the letter Siegfried wrote to the Prince of Saxe-Altdorf. There was a vague reference to Siegfried's clandestine departure, but he returned to France unhindered—and asleep. The brilliant writing of those last pages describing Jean's arrival in France compensated somewhat for what was in fact an anticlimactic dénouement, but in the dramatic adaptation Giraudoux could not escape so easily from a forthright solution to the plot.

Events subsequent to the composition of the novel, such as the assassination of Walter Rathenau, Minister of Foreign Affairs, in 1922 and the Munich Putsch of 1923, suggested a tragic ending for *Siegfried von Kleist*. This is prepared by a farcical scene at the beginning of Act IV between two masked men, who are walking about in the gallery of Nymphenbourg Castle, the residence of the Prince of Saxe-Altdorf. From their conversation we learn that they are two assassins who have been summoned to the castle to kill Siegfried, but it is not clear whether they have been sent by the Prince or by the generals. The setting for the last act is taken from the piece entitled *Visite chez le Prince* (1923) in which we first encountered General Fontgeloy. Siegfried has come to this picturesque spot, not far from Munich and near a settlement of French Huguenots, who manufacture Limoges china, to seek political asylum in the home of this urbane and courtly prince. Siegfried is accompanied by Geneviève and Robineau. It is the latter who pleads Siegfried's case and who explains that Zelten has publicly exposed the latter's French nationality. The Prince does not seem in any way surprised and requests to see Siegfried. Robineau has already informed the Prince of Siegfried's intention to leave the country, and Siegfried himself elaborates on the plan. Since Robineau and Geneviève had both been warned that Siegfried would never be allowed to leave Germany alive, his escape is being covered by a false report of his death issued by Generals Waldorf and Fontgeloy. The Prince seems to listen with sympathy to this plan, and he even points out the service Siegfried could perform for his countrymen by revealing to the French the true face of Germany. It is curious that Giraudoux has the Prince utter words which he later repeated in the program of the final version of the play, *Siegfried*:

> You know what I think about our two countries. The question of harmony between them is the only serious question in the universe. . . . All the ills of Europe stem from the fact that France is in ignorance of Germany. When one lives near a country perpetually impelled to paroxysm, to delusions of grandeur, to a brutal love of the whole world, one must not leave that country alone for a minute. It must be harassed, worried, closely watched.[25]

Although the Prince is the author's mouthpiece, it is difficult to believe that he is not in league with the generals or that he has any intention of giving back to France "the bold foreigner who has seen Germany naked." In any event, he makes no effort either to warn or to protect Siegfried. After a touching scene with Geneviève, Siegfried excuses himself to go for a walk in the park, where the two murderers await him. A bullet strikes him in the same place as the one which wounded him six years earlier. Siegfried is brought in on a stretcher by the Nymphenbourg porcelain makers. When he regains consciousness, his memory has returned; and it is Jacques Forestier who speaks, believing that he is near the front. There is another exchange between him and Geneviève, whom he finally recognizes as the woman he has loved; but he is unaware of his surroundings or of the second life he has led as Siegfried von Kleist. The doctor arrives just in time to pronounce the final words of the play: "Er ist gestorben."

This sudden and violent end to the career of Siegfried does not exploit the psychological possibilities of the plot as Anouilh was to do some years later in *Le Voyageur sans bagages* (1936),

[25] *Fin de Siegfried, Théâtre complet*, I, 184. See also p. 57.

but it has a dramatic and emotional power of which Giraudoux was justly proud. What the closing scene loses in psychological interest, it gains in political significance, for the French soldier dies prophetically a second time at the hands of the German militarists before he can realize what has struck him. Furthermore, the symbolism is dual, for the violent death of Jacques Forestier is at the same time the end of Siegfried, the symbol of the German Republic, in which the Allies had placed their hopes for world peace.

On the whole, *Siegfried von Kleist* conveys the author's message with clarity. The style is subordinate to the idea, or perhaps it would be more accurate to say that the style sets off the ideas instead of obscuring them as in the novel. Not that the dialogue is rapid or familiar. On the contrary, there are many long speeches, full of those acrobatics which often leave us breathless at the end of a sentence. Nevertheless, the author's line of thought seems less tortuous than in the novel, and the scenes of exposition prepare logically for the unfolding of the dramatic action. This time Giraudoux really pursued the problem and "awakened the old boy," as he said in an interview.[26] In the many changes of scene from the Munich boardinghouse to Siegfried's office to the picturesque settings of the Wittelsbach palace and the Nymphenbourg castle and by the verve with which he mingles the tragic and the comic, Giraudoux is already showing a Shakespearean vein of dramatic talent, which will inevitably be disciplined to conform to the classical unities of time, place, and action. In this first manuscript which Giraudoux brought to Jouvet, the experienced man of the theatre recognized the mark of a great dramatist, but before he was willing to produce the play, it underwent serious modifications both in substance and in form.

[26] *Paris Midi,* May 1, 1928.

IV

Siegfried

The play *Siegfried* which opened at the Champs-Elysées Theatre on May 3, 1928 is a literary and dramatic accomplishment which in some respects Giraudoux never surpassed. On this point the critics are agreed, but as in the case of *Siegfried et le Limousin,* they have evaded serious discussion of the political content of the work. Giraudoux complained of this,[1] with what justification we shall soon see. Between *Siegfried von Kleist* and the final version of the play there were innumerable revisions,[2] due in part to the exigencies of the theatre and in part to the change in the political wind. Giraudoux's original idea is reduced to the following scenario: Siegfried, a victim of amnesia in search of his past, is the great counselor and hope of the new Germany; Zelten, his political rival, is fully prepared to expose Siegfried's French origin to the Parliament; Eva, the symbol of Siegfried's new mother country, wants to conceal Siegfried's identity in order to keep him in Germany; Geneviève, the symbol of his French past, wants to cure Siegfried and return him to France; Zelten attempts a *coup d'état* which fails, but before his abdication he reveals the fact that Siegfried is a foreigner sup-

---

[1] In an interview for *L'Intransigeant,* August 9, 1928. See also p. 59.
[2] In Albérès' study of *La Genèse de Siegfried,* he compares several manuscript versions and gives a detailed account of the various stages the play went through before arriving at its final form. He does not, however, discuss the political signification of these changes.

ported by foreign capital; Eva and Geneviève vie for Siegfried's affections; Siegfried flees to the border, but the polite intervention of his generals and a subtle shift in Geneviève's position persuade him to remain in Germany. In short, Franco-German relations are evoked by an engaging flirtation between a Frenchwoman and a German statesman.

In this streamlined version the political symbolism has become so generalized that it does not lend itself readily to rational analysis without knowledge of the sources of the play. Eva has been cleansed of her associations with the hate societies; only Fontgeloy remains to suggest the threat of Prussian militarism. The supporters of Siegfried and Zelten are named only by implication. The moral of the play has been even more seriously modified. Zelten, although telling the truth, is a traitor to Germany; Siegfried, the impostor, who does not represent the true face of Germany, is indispensable to his adoptive country; and France, though mindful of the past, will try to love and uphold her sister Republic. These are conclusions that are consistent with public opinion in 1928, but they represent many concessions on the part of Giraudoux.

The publication of *Siegfried et le Limousin* came a few years after the birth of the German Republic, which from the very beginning was recognized as a sort of subterfuge intended to win the confidence of Europe and to obtain more favorable peace terms. The situation within Germany had not changed perceptibly between 1922 and 1928; but after Germany entered the League of Nations in 1926, Europe had to put trust in her, at least officially. The point that Giraudoux made very well in *Siegfried von Kleist* is that the confidence of the Allies was misplaced. He brought to Jouvet a sincere manuscript in which he tried to expose the true face of Germany to his over-optimistic compatriots. Jouvet's critical mind recognized the literary and dramatic merits of the text, but the many changes of scene, the large cast of characters, and the complexity of the ideas which Giraudoux was trying to express, presented problems for the director. The play needed a great deal of pruning to achieve that unity of tone and action which French taste requires of good theatre. Whether Jouvet himself took issue with the melodramatic dénouement is a matter of conjecture. It was certainly a bit risky to run counter to public opinion by sounding like a prophet of doom when the olive branch had just been extended. In order to assure a good reception, it seemed wise to slant the whole thing a bit differently. Jouvet had recently been involved in an unfortunate venture, the production of Crommelynck's *Tripes d'or* (1925). This satire on the cult of the Golden Calf had shocked the public as much by its bad taste as by its boldness. The result was an expensive failure which Jouvet could not afford to repeat. It is therefore probable that he imposed his own terms on the inexperienced playwright and gave him to understand that the theatre demands as much discretion as the diplomatic service. After all, independent theatre is a commercial enterprise, which has its financial risks like any other. A director is perfectly free to defy the critics and go bankrupt if he chooses, but his freedom can never go beyond the limits of his financial backing. In the case of *Siegfried,* it took much courage to produce the first play of a writer as difficult as Giraudoux, to say nothing of compounding the risk by presenting controversial ideas. It seems likely, then, that a good many of the modifications of the original text were dictated not only by the rules of dramatic structure but also by the proprieties of 1928.

The first obvious change is in the time and place of the final version. The action of *Siegfried* unfolds in Gotha, not in Munich, and Zelten gives the date of his revolution as January 13 or 14, 1921. The discrepancy, in the novel and in the adaptation, between the historical date of these Bolshevist uprisings and the date given by the author has already been pointed out. In the final version it was necessary to avoid this discrepancy in one way or another. Rather than reveal the original source of his work and admit that it dealt with "the terror in Bavaria," Giraudoux chose a more obscure Communist uprising, which took place in Gotha in the month of March 1921, following demonstrations provoked by the anniversary of the deaths of Rosa Luxembourg and Karl Liebknecht.[3] The town of Gotha offered certain advantages over Munich, one of which is the fact that it is situated in Thuringia, very near Weimar, seat of the National Assembly. Therefore, when Siegfried returns triumphantly from Parliament, which has just voted to adopt his constitution, it is more logical that the action of the play unfold in Gotha, where the opposition between the Weimar Republic and Bolshevism has a certain geographical probability. Since the constitution was adopted in 1919 and not in 1921, Giraudoux is still taking liberties with historical fact; but Siegfried and his constitution are, after all, Giraudoux's own creation, whereas he could not tamper with the date of Eisner's death and the events that followed. Gotha offers another advantage as well—perhaps a purely fortuitous one. The town is known for its *Almanac,* a genealogical, diplomatic, and statistical directory published yearly in French and German since 1763. This makes Gotha an appropriate setting for the Franco-German association which is embodied in the character Siegfried. In short, this first modification corrects certain inconsistencies in the original text and is more suitable to the change in political orientation. It heightens the role of Siegfried by associating him more closely with the Weimar Constitution, while playing down the role of Zelten by removing him from the scene of the notorious Munich uprisings.

Not only did Giraudoux effect a change in the time and place of *Siegfried,* but he went on to change the setting of three out of the four acts of the play. Gone is the Munich boardinghouse,

[3] See the *New York Times,* March 30, 1921, 1:6.

which in any event was a little too reminiscent of the boulevard comedy; gone is the comic opera setting of the throne room of the Wittelsbach palace; gone is the picturesque gallery and park of the Nymphenbourg Castle. The only setting that remains of *Siegfried von Kleist* is Siegfried's office, which is the scene of the first three acts in the final version. This would seem to be a concession to the classic tradition of unity of place, and it has the customary effect of reducing most of the action to talk. The first act soberly presents the four protagonists—Siegfried and Zelten, Eva and Geneviève—with Robineau acting as a go-between. Gone are the caricature, the farce, and the spies. Everyone is polite and well behaved; there is no hint of bad faith or foul play. The second act reports on Zelten's revolution and the efforts of Eva and Fontgeloy to dissuade him from unmasking Siegfried. In the third act Zelten reappears to confront Siegfried after the session of Parliament, then leaves him to Eva and Geneviève.

The main outline of the plot in these first three acts does not differ essentially from that of *Siegfried von Kleist,* but the action unfolds not only with a greater economy of stage sets but also with a much smaller cast of characters. Such key personages as Schmeck, Liévine Liéven, and the Prince of Saxe-Altdorf have been eliminated from the final version, and the remaining ones are considerably less colorful and complex. Robineau is still a philologian, but in changing the scene from Munich to Gotha, Giraudoux sacrificed the major part of that first scene which came from the homage to Andler. The arrival of Robineau and Geneviève in Germany becomes the fifth scene of the final version. It serves solely as an introduction and has lost its elements of farce and caricature. Similarly, the elimination of the role of Liévine Liéven removes the more objectionable satire from the character of Robineau. As for Geneviève, there is no longer any hint of her Bohemian past. Her eccentricities have been eliminated, and her role is primarily that of the straightforward and rather touching fiancée of Jacques Forestier. Eva's role is equally straightforward; she is no longer the symbol of a revengeful Germany. While she is still in league with Fontgeloy, the latter is considerably less menacing in this version, even though he is introduced as being one of the fourteen generals, the thirty-two colonels, and the three hundred army officers of French descent who were the backbone of the Prussian Army in 1914, according to Giraudoux.

The exposition of the political conflict between Zelten and Siegfried is much more subtle in the final version. The curtain goes up on the antichamber of Siegfried's office in Gotha. Muck is still there to keep watch at the door, but this time he plays a straight role. He merely announces General von Ludendorff and President Rathenau, who never actually appear on stage; but the very mention of their names evokes the two powers upholding the Republic—the army and the moneyed interests. These illustrious gentlemen are obliged to wait while Siegfried receives a crowd of ordinary people, who arrive from the four corners of Germany in the hope of recognizing him as a son lost in the war. This scene is similar to that of the first version in which Muck announced General von Ludendorff and Marshal von Hindenburg directly after Eva had assured Siegfried that one day he would find his mother. The same symbolism is apparent here, modified by the substitution of Rathenau for Hindenburg. Giraudoux, understandably enough, had some second thoughts about naming the current President of the German Republic in the stage version of his play. Moreover, the name of Ludendorff was sufficient to suggest the military caste which had brought Hindenburg to power. The name of Rathenau, a big industrialist, recalls one of Siegfried's French prototypes, Dumas, prime minister of the steel kingdom.[4] Rathenau presided not

[4] See p. 41.

over Parliament but over the administrative offices of the big corporations. He is the first in a long line of similar presidents who people Giraudoux's plays until they rush into the trap set for them by the Madwoman of Chaillot. The allusion to Rathenau, who died a violent death at the hands of the reactionaries he served, foreshadows the tragic dénouement that Giraudoux originally envisioned for his play.

The major part of the exposition is furnished by Eva and Zelten in the second scene. Zelten attacks Siegfried's plan for a constitution, using the familiar metaphor of the dragon and the alarm clock, but his own position appears even more absurd than in the earlier version. He favors bringing back the fragmented Germany of the Holy Empire, with its little kingdoms and duchies because, as he says, "Germany is not a social and human enterprise, but a poetic and demoniac conjuration."[5] Actually, Zelten's predilection for the political divisions of the Holy Empire is a euphemistic statement of a policy of separatism advocated in certain allied circles and by some German liberals as a means of preventing a resurgence of German militarism. Forester, for example, was opposed to the centralization of the Reich, but Giraudoux attributes this position to Zelten rather than to Siegfried, having consistently portrayed the former as the true friend of France. Robineau, who in *Siegfried von Kleist* had emphasized Zelten's generosity and his friendship for France, in the final version portrays Zelten primarily as an esthete and an eccentric. What we have seen of Zelten thus far in Act I seems to bear out Robineau's prewar recollection of him. However, in the following scene when Zelten and Robineau are face to face for the first time since the war, Zelten becomes more explicit about his aims and activities. "I am fighting against the real enemies of Germany," he explains to Robineau. "Countries are like fruit: the worms are always in-

[5] *Théâtre complet,* I, p. 14.

side." When Robineau, dumbfounded, asks him whether he is propagandizing, Zelten replies, "No, I am starting a revolution. Today is the twelfth of January, 1921. My revolution will take place from the thirteenth to the fourteenth of January, 1921" (p. 30). This date corresponds to the anniversary of the Spartacist revolution, which took place from the fifth to the fifteenth of January, 1919.[6] In spite of the precise reference to time, which gives a hint of Zelten's political leanings, no critic, to my knowledge, took the author seriously enough to inquire what Zelten's revolution was intended to represent.

In the second act Zelten's revolution seems to be no more than a demonstration. "The Communists?" asks Fontgeloy. "No, Zelten," Eva replies. This is what might be called identification by association. The bit of dialogue that follows is no more informative. Fontgeloy is addressing Geneviève in the presence of Eva: "Madame, although a foreigner, had the privilege yesterday of meeting here, within the same hour, the two faces of Germany—Zelten and Siegfried." Eva elaborates with the cryptic remark: "One is true, Madame. The other is a mask" (p. 67). This statement can be interpreted with some certainty after extensive exegesis, but the critics of 1928 would have needed a talent for divination to have understood it. "These demonstrations of cocain addicts and cubists," as Fontgeloy describes them, represent the thirty million German leftists of whom Schmeck speaks in *Siegfried von Kleist.* Siegfried, with his plan for a republican constitution, is a mask that hides the other thirty million Germans who hate France and are plotting a war of revenge. However, this aspect of Siegfried is no longer apparent because of the omission of Schmeck and the discretion of Fontgeloy in the final version.

Act III shows Zelten waiting for Siegfried to return from the session of Parliament. Zelten has just escaped from the two

[6] See pp. 43, 84.

soldiers who guarded the door of his room, but he does not arrive in time to denounce Siegfried before the Parliament. When Siegfried enters, accompanied by his generals, the confrontation scene is a literary and dramatic masterpiece. But despite Zelten's spirited and eloquent defense and the zeal he displays in unmasking his adversary, the spectator may well wonder what the excitement is all about. The Parliament has just voted Zelten's exile, a move which Zelten explains, as he did in the novel and *Siegfried von Kleist,* by the interception of the telegrams. Having thus demonstrated that Germany's choice of government is dictated by foreign powers, he announces that this is his last effort to prevent his country from becoming a combine. This much is consistent with the previous version, but Zelten's action in *Siegfried* is purely negative; he is never given an opportunity to present his own program, an alliance with France and the electrification of the country for the benefit of all the people. Consequently, Zelten seems to be more an anarchist than anything else in this emasculated version. If he is intended to represent the true face of Germany, the image is so blurred and shadowy that the public could not be expected to be much enlightened by it. The unmasking of Siegfried does not reveal anything really significant either, unless the spectator's powers of inference are remarkably strong. Like Zelten's connection with the Communists, Siegfried's association with the militarists and the big corporations is indicated only by indirection. One can assume that Fontgeloy and Eva were responsible for preventing Zelten from appearing before the Parliament, and that Siegfried's government thus has the backing of the most reactionary military forces as well as that of the big corporations. But the diplomat of 1928 was less eager to clarify these issues than was the novice playwright of 1926.

In the closing scenes of Act III, the dramatic interest shifts from the political conflict between Siegfried and Zelten to the psychological effect of the discovery of Siegfried's true identity. Siegfried is torn between the appeals of the two women who represent his dual nationality. He has still not recovered his memory, so that the past of Jacques Forestier has no reality for him until Geneviève strikes the right note at last by evoking the image of a white poodle waiting for his master to return. In the end Geneviève's argument has more effect than Eva's call to duty and her veiled threats. It is also more compelling than the news item about the collision of two freight cars of elephants in a French railway station, which Giraudoux used in the novel and the original version of the play to evoke the country of Siegfried's origin.

The last act of *Siegfried,* which must decide his political future and resolve the dilemma of his dual nationality, is situated most appropriately in a frontier railroad station. This is a welcome change from the classic simplicity of Siegfried's office, and with it comes a welcome touch of light comedy as well. Robineau pokes sly fun at the customs officer, Pietri, whose witticism regarding the insularity of the French has already become a proverb:

ROBINEAU: Tell me, customs officer, why is it that all the customs officers in France are Corsican?

PIETRI: Because it takes a Corsican to understand that France is an island.

To all appearances, the stage is set for the return of Siegfried to France, when Generals Waldorf and Ledinger arrive. They make a polite but futile attempt to persuade Siegfried to remain in Germany. Unlike Fontgeloy, their persuasion is not accompanied by threats, but one can detect the same note of warning which the Prince of Saxe-Altdorf voiced in the earlier version: "Think of that mask which all the French wear, that mask which prevents them from inhaling the noxious gases of Europe,

but which often impedes their breathing and blocks their sight."
To which Siegfried replies: "I shall be the barefaced Frenchman, the counterpart of the German without a memory" (p.
119). Thus it would seem that Siegfried's mission, since he can
no longer serve Germany in all good conscience, is to caution
the French against a rebirth of German militarism. Again the
implication is so subtle that the author's meaning becomes clear
only by comparison with the earlier version. Sensing this, Giraudoux reiterated his warning in the program notes of the play by
quoting from another fragment of the Siegfried cycle, *"Visite
chez le Prince."*[7]

If Giraudoux deliberately played down his original meaning
in the final text, it is because the times demanded a more positive approach to the Franco-German problem and forced him to
revise completely the tragic dénouement. If he had allowed Siegfried to return unharmed to France, as in the novel, the whole
dramatic action would have collapsed. Not without difficulty,
Giraudoux finally hit upon a better solution. First, he relieved
the tension by another comic exchange, this time between Geneviève and the customs officer. Then, just as one is expecting Siegfried and Geneviève to board the train, there is a reversal. Up to
this point, Siegfried has still not recovered his memory; the
sentimental theme is therefore at an impasse. Geneviève has no
immediate hope of regaining the affection of the Frenchman,
Jacques Forestier, but in her capacity as tutor and confidant she
has learned to love his German counterpart. She chooses this
moment to declare her love and her acceptance of his other life
by detaining him on the German side of the frontier with the
words: "Siegfried, je t'aime." This Hollywood ending is as symbolic in its way as the more solemn words of *Siegfried von
Kleist:* "Er ist gestorben."

Given the general state of mind in 1928, it is not at all cer-

[7] See pp. 57, 79.

tain that *Siegfried* would have had the same resounding success if Giraudoux had not made this concession to public opinion. But when he saw fascism take over in Germany and the fascists attempt a *coup d'état* even in France, Giraudoux could no longer keep silent. It is significant that he published the original version of his fourth act in *Les Nouvelles Littéraires,* not after Hitler took power, but after the fascist riots broke out in France on February 6, 1934. Giraudoux introduced it by saying that he was "today publishing this fantasy, for which, in fact, current events provide exactly the right setting."[8] The following year he found the courage to produce a play with an uncompromising and truly prophetic ending, *La Guerre de Troie n'aura pas lieu,* which had the sort of impact on the public of its time that Giraudoux had doubtless intended for his *Siegfried.*

Giraudoux's conscience may have suffered a few pangs when he saw the curtain go down on that saccharine dénouement, but there were no regrets at the box office. The play ran through 302 performances, a record that has never been surpassed by any other play in Giraudoux's repertoire, with the exception of *Ondine.* The critics, who were baffled by the fanciful style of Giraudoux's novels, were prepared for a magnificent flop. Instead they were greeted by an evening of brilliant theatre such as Paris had not seen since the *ancien régime.* Any reservations the critics might have had were swept away by the acclaim of that first night audience. The press, flabbergasted, grudgingly did obeisance. A critic who responded rather coldly at the time later gave a fairly accurate account of the effect produced by *Siegfried* when it was first performed:

> Overnight Giraudoux ceased being of interest only to bibliophiles and became an object of public discussion. That represented a conquest which justified raising the flags. Letters had come back to the theatre, and not timidly, but through the front gates. You

[8] "Suite à Siegfried," *Nouvelles Littéraires,* August 11, 18, 25, 1934.

were offered, with the glitter of the old boulevard, something other than Bernstein, or Louis Verneuil or Sacha Guitry. The friends of dramatic art could quiver with happiness and hope.[9]

The public was delighted to see on stage, couched in Giraudoux's elegant badinage, a reflection of its own deep-seated worries and its hopes for the peace of Europe. But Giraudoux was not satisfied to shine as a playwright; he would have liked to compel recognition as a thinker. According to his press interviews, Giraudoux's intentions in *Siegfried* were polemical. An analysis of the Siegfried cycle has shown that the author saw Germany as a country torn between two extremist groups, and the German Republic as a government imposed by the Allies to crush the Bolshevist uprisings. Meanwhile, he felt strongly that the Republic was being used by the extreme right to protect and mask the forces most dangerous to the future peace of Europe. However, by portraying Bolshevism in the guise of the esthetic and eccentric Zelten, who pleads guilty to committing an act of adultery with Germany—for it is thus that he describes his attempt to overthrow Siegfried's government—by making an amnesic French soldier the symbol of the German Republic, and by depicting Franco-German relations as a love affair interrupted by war, Giraudoux has indeed created a new form of polemic. Could he in all good faith reproach the critics of 1928 for their reluctance to discuss the subject of his play?

Giraudoux's first success in the theatre is not unlike that of his Agnès in *L'Apollon de Bellac,* a one-act play which Giraudoux wrote during the Occupation. Agnès is a young girl with no money and no skills. Though she is very attractive, she is afraid

[9] Pierre Brisson, *Le Théatre des années folles* (1934), p. 56. In 1928 Pierre Brisson was drama critic for *Le Temps.* He later became editor of *Le Figaro.* He never expressed much enthusiasm for Giraudoux's theatre, so that this tribute may reflect the force of public opinion rather than his own sentiments. It was Benjamin Crémieux of *Les Nouvelles Littéraires* who was Giraudoux's best critic.

of men. She is looking for employment; but without the advice of the Gentleman from Bellac, she would have had difficulty surviving in this cruel world. This gentleman teaches her to look a man straight in the eye and tell him that he is handsome. With this formula, he assures her, she can have anything she wants. Under his tutelage she first wins the heart of the receptionist, who ushers her into the Secretary General's office. He, too, falls under the charm of her magic formula and introduces her to the President. The President offers her a diamond and marriage. Agnès is dazzled by her success, but not entirely satisfied. "The fact of repeating your phrase," she says to the Gentleman of Bellac, "has given me a special desire . . . I feel ripe for telling someone really handsome that he is handsome; I need that reward and that punishment."[10] But when she must choose between supreme beauty and the President's diamond, she decides in favor of the diamond, saying: "Don't count on me too much, supreme beauty. You know, I have an ordinary little life. My daily tasks are mediocre, and when I get back to my room, I have five flights to climb in semi-darkness and the smell of cooking fat. . . . That is my life! It is made up of shadows and crushed, slightly bruised flesh. That is my conscience: it's a stairway. So if I'm reluctant to imagine you as you are, it is in my own defense. Don't hold it against me . . . " (p. 193). One can imagine Giraudoux pleading his own case in the words of Agnès, for it was Louis Jouvet who inspired the role of the Gentleman from Bellac. The identification between this actor-director, who guided the novice playwright to his first success, and the Gentleman from Bellac was so complete in the author's mind that he originally assigned Jouvet's name to that character,[11] and it was probably Jouvet himself who later substituted the name of the Gentleman from Bellac, which identi-

---

[10] *Théâtre complet,* XVI, 190.
[11] *Visitations* (Paris and Neuchâtel: Ides et Calendes, 1947), pp. 23–25.

fies the character with Giraudoux by the reference to the author's birthplace. The name of Agnès recalls Molière's heroine of *L'École des Femmes,* which Louis Jouvet directed with such success shortly before the war. One might guess that the Agnès of Giraudoux's play is the inexperienced playwright, who succeeds, thanks to Jouvet's advice. Like Agnès, Giraudoux had a vision of supreme beauty, but being poor and timid, he preferred the kind of reward that he could see and touch.

At the time that Giraudoux was writing his *Siegfried,* he looked upon the theatre as an assembly hall where the crowd gathers to meditate on great problems. After the defeat of 1940, he saw the theatre as a radiant confessional where "the crowd comes . . . to listen to its own confessions of cowardice and sacrifice, hate and passion."[12] *L'Apollon de Bellac* is his first public confession of this kind. In *Sodome et Gomorrhe* there are others graver in tone and wider in scope.

[12] *Ibid.,* pp. 127–28.

After the Defeat

THEATER OF THE OCCUPATION

V

Sodome et Gomorrhe

The first performance of *Sodome et Gomorrhe* took place on October 11, 1943, at the Théâtre Hébertot, while France was still in the throes of the German Occupation. Despite the presence of the Nazis, the year 1943 offered a brilliant theatrical season with Claudel's *Soulier de Satin,* Jean Anouilh's *Antigone,* Sartre's *Les Mouches,* and Montherlant's *La Reine Morte,* but the most talked-about work of the season was that of Jean Giraudoux. This was the first time that the author of *Siegfried* had brought his political meditations before the public since the days of the "phony war," when in his capacity as minister of propaganda he was an official commentator on Franco-German relations. Given the circumstances, one would not expect Giraudoux to break a two-year silence only to voice banalities. On the other hand, any artist who produced under the German Occupation had to reckon with Nazi censorship. However, censorship from one source or another seems to be an ever-present problem with which Giraudoux had grappled before with varying degrees of success. If he had something to say, he, better than anyone else, could find a way to say it even under Nazi surveillance.

The title of the play was sufficient to suggest that the subject would have some analogy with the defeat of 1940. The Old Testament story in which God destroyed the two cities of Sodom and Gomorrah by fire from heaven because of their depravity may have been in the mind of Marshal Pétain when he addressed the French at the time of the armistice of June 25, 1940: "Our defeat is the result of our laxity. The spirit of pleasure is destroying what the spirit of sacrifice built up. What I bid you, first of all, is to effect an intellectual and moral recovery."[1]

The Six Weeks' War, which ended so abruptly and irrevocably in defeat and occupation, created a state of mind in France that was conducive to some soul-searching even without the admonition of the Marshal, who seemed to be placing the blame for the disaster upon the entire nation. With the possible exception of *Pour Lucrèce,* a play which was not made public until 1953, all of Giraudoux's writings during this period reflect his reaction to the Marshal's public utterances. The publication of Pétain's speeches in book form in 1941 may actually have triggered the composition of *Sodome et Gomorrhe.* We know that Giraudoux began work on the play in 1941, for he spoke of it in a lecture he gave in Switzerland in February 1942, remarking sardonically that that winter he had attacked a fairly rough subject, the end of the world, that is to say the destruction of Sodom and Gomorrah.[2] Although the play was not produced until the fall of 1943, he had already finished writing it by May 1942, according to a note which he made on the first page of the manuscript of *L'Apollon de Bellac* when he sent it to Louis Jouvet.[3]

Sodome et Gomorrhe opens with a long prelude in which the Archangel of Archangels warns the spectator that he is about to witness a frightful spectacle, the end of the world; that is to say, the collapse of a civilization. While the presence of the Arch-

[1] "Appel du 25 juin 1940," *La France nouvelle* (Paris: Fasquelle, 1941), p. 26.

[2] *Visitations* (Neuchatel et Paris: Ides et Calendes, 1947), p. 102.

[3] See the program of *L'Apollon de Bellac.* Louis Jouvet was in Rio de Janeiro at this time and produced the play there.

angel is in keeping with the Biblical text, his speech is sprinkled with anachronisms that evoke the fall of France. And the Archangel speaks with a curious mixture of levity and solemnity that is reminiscent of Giraudoux's radio addresses shortly before the war. In fact, the Archangel and the Angel in *Sodome et Gomorrhe* bear a certain resemblance to "the archangels and lesser angels of the Information Service" who "have nothing in common with the truth but nakedness."[4] The Archangel's exposition of the subject of the play is as straightforward and informative as a heavily censored news broadcast:

> At the zenith of invention and talent, in the intoxicating fulness of life and exploitation of the world, at a time when the army is fine and new, the wine cellars full, the theatres resounding; and when the dyers discover purple and pure white, when diamonds are discovered in the mines, and in the cells atoms, and when out of the air we make symphonies and out of the seas health; when a thousand methods have been found to protect pedestrians from cars, and remedies for cold and night and ugliness; at a time when all alliances protect us from war . . . suddenly, in a few hours, a disease attacks this healthiest and happiest of bodies. It is the disease of empires . . . It is fatal . . . The disease springs up in the very place where it was wiped out forever, the wolf in the heart of the city, the louse on the cranium of the multi-millionaire. My colleague, the archangel who curdles the cream and the sauces in the kitchen of empires, has entered, and the end has come.[5]

This eloquent but cavalier treatment of such a grave subject is disconcerting, to say the least, and what follows is even more so. When the Archangel gives his diagnosis of the disease of empires, attributing it to the dissolution of the couple, to the fact that men and women can no longer live together in love and

---

[4] *Sans Pouvoirs* (Monaco: Editions du Rocher, 1946), p. 89.
[5] *Théâtre Complet*, X, 10.

harmony and prefer to go their separate ways, one begins to wonder if the author has become a *Pétainiste* or a fundamentalist. As the dialogue unfolds—one can hardly call it a plot—the levity disappears and the spectator is subjected to two long acts of conjugal discord, which even the wrath of God is not able to silence. This is a far cry from *Amphitryon 38* (1929), that joyous hymn to marital fidelity which followed *Siegfried* and which, ironically enough, had been made into an opera by Marcel Bertrand that was playing at the Opéra-Comique concurrently with *Sodome et Gomorrhe* at the Théâtre Hébertot. Even the end of the world, which seems to be nothing more than a backdrop for the drama of the battle of the sexes, hardly explains the particular manner in which Giraudoux chose to develop his subject. Yet, if we recall the ironic observation he made in his essay on Racine,[6] that the French are a people for whom public and romantic tragedies are rather rare and who reserve their passion for domestic differences, it is not surprising to see France's darkest moment eclipsed in the play by the misunderstanding between man and woman, "the most fascinating and serious conflict of life and of the stage."[7] Though Giraudoux's preoccupation with this theme seems to be in the French classical tradition, it also doubtless reflects a crisis in his own domestic life, which seemed to parallel the national crisis. The cause-and-effect relationship, however, hardly represents the kind of thinking that one would expect from one of the most sophisticated of twentieth-century writers and diplomats, unless one is to conclude that he seriously embraced the political philosophy of the New Order, whose motto WORK, FAMILY, and COUNTRY had made LIBERTY, EQUALITY, and FRATERNITY obsolete.

The apparent subject of the play, as Giraudoux depicts it in the drama of the perfect couple, Jean and Lia, supported by two

---

[6] *Littérature,* p. 50.
[7] *Visitations,* p. 47.

minor couples, Ruth and Jacques, and Samson and Delilah, is the incompatibility of the sexes, which is undermining the very foundations of society. Their dissension is portrayed with such virulence that the spectator all but comes to the conclusion that man and woman were not made to live together, that society leans towards homosexuality, and that this merits the end of the world. More than one critic[8] accepted the thesis of the play at its face value. This is not so preposterous as it may seem if one recalls that the vice of the Biblical cities had its parallel in the literary world between the two wars. As one critic put it, "Since Proust, the cause of freedom tends to be confused with the cause of pederasty."[9] This could be said with even more justice in reference to Gide. The homosexual was becoming a familiar character in plays as well as novels. Even Giraudoux portrayed one such in his play *Judith,* apropos of which a drama critic made the withering remark that he prayed God to spare him his nightly pederast.[10] There is thus a certain mischievous logic on the part of Giraudoux in identifying the Paris of the Occupation with the fate of Sodom and Gomorrah, a logic which was also in keeping with the Marshal's exhortation to effect an intellectual and moral recovery. The censors as well as the critics were content to accept a literal interpretation of the play. At least we have no knowledge that Giraudoux or the management of the Théâtre Hébertot experienced any difficulty with censorship. But given the historical moment and the audience for which the play was written, it is reasonable to assume that things are not quite what they seem and to inquire into Giraudoux's real attitude toward the defeat.

[8] This was the conclusion of the press and of Jacques Houlet, *Le Théâtre de Giraudoux* (Paris: Pierre Ardent, 1945), p. 117.

[9] Emmanuel Berl, *La Mort de la pensée bourgeoise* (Paris: Grasset, 1929), p. 82.

[10] Lugné-Poë in his review of *Judith* in *L'Avenir,* November 6, 1931.

As a matter of fact, Giraudoux was far from accepting Pétain's version of the fall of France. His immediate reaction to the capitulation and Pétain's pious *mea culpa* on behalf of the French nation is recorded in a booklet, published posthumously, entitled *Armistice à Bordeaux*.[11] As the Armistice was about to be signed Giraudoux wrote: "In three-quarters of an hour the war will be taken out of the hands of the French. 'Tis a pity. A war in which France has no part will always lack a kind of honor. . . . Our honor is not one of laurel and sycamore; it consists in having been swindled, castigated, thrashed, either for our vices or for our virtues, but in never having confused, even when it was in our favor, the judgment of sabers with the Last Judgment" (pp. 13, 43). This booklet, which might well serve as a foreword to the play, makes no mention of the moral laxity of the nation, to which Pétain attributed the defeat of France.

Giraudoux spelled out his feelings even more clearly in *Visitations,* a lecture he gave in Switzerland eight months after the armistice at Bordeaux. He illustrated his lecture with several short scenes from the plays that he was working on at the time. Among these is a scene that links *Armistice à Bordeaux* with *Sodome et Gomorrhe* via the gardener, whom the author describes as "that indefatigable commentator . . . on the upheavals of the world."[12] The gardener made his first appearance in *Electre* (1937), and he appears again in the prelude to *Sodome et Gomorrhe*. This mysterious character is clearly identified with the author, who describes thus the scene he is about to present in *Visitations:* "The setting is a garden. The gardener is seated near the son of the house, who angrily unfolds a newspaper in which it is said that every Frenchman is responsible for the disaster" (p. 93). The gardener speaks, and it is significant that

[11] Neuchâtel: Ides et Calendes, 1945.
[12] *Visitations*, p. 85.

these words were penned at the same time that the author was composing *Sodome et Gomorrhe:*

> You're right, don't give in. Do like me. Don't go admitting your guilt in this catastrophe. This confession of guilt which they are asking of us, refuse it, like me. Leave it to those who are responsible. It is now, on the contrary, that I see clearly that I have not sinned, that I have had no hand in this disaster. . . . You haven't sinned either, that is plain. . . . You'll see. Everything will be all right. There are thousands like us on whom repentance, even today, has no hold; hope is reviving. (pp. 94–96)

This passage was incorporated into *Armistice à Bordeaux,* where it was preceded by the prophetic promise: "Yes, that's how we'll avenge ourselves for the blame and the dishonor: we shall one day force the universe to see, by our resistance, that we who fled personify audacity anew, that we who have denied our faith personify faith anew, and that from this horrible taste in our mouths and in our minds we shall make again the salt of the earth" (p. 37). These words were addressed to Giraudoux's son, who was mobilized as an infantryman in June 1940 and who joined the Free French Naval Forces after the armistice. Two months later, Jean-Pierre Giraudoux was broadcasting from London echoes of this conversation.

Giraudoux's reactions to the defeat are revealed in an even more important text which he was preparing during the Occupation as a companion piece to his prewar political work *Pleins Pouvoirs.* It bears the appropriate title *Sans Pouvoirs* and was published posthumously and unfinished. Here, too, Giraudoux makes very clear that he did not subscribe to the principle of the leaders at Vichy, which was, as he expressed it, "to make this universal drama into a case against our average citizen" and to make "every individual Frenchman assume the total responsibility for a disaster whose roots pushed far out into other continents" (p. 14). As Pétain was pontificating: "Let us learn the lesson of lost battles. Since our victory, the spirit of pleasure has prevailed over the spirit of sacrifice,"[13] Giraudoux was replying in *Sans Pouvoirs:* ". . . at this hour, as I write from the very bottom of the abyss, it is my most rigorous duty to point out that none of their mottoes has been accepted by the country and that the lesson of events is, for France, very far from the truths in which certain leaders have claimed to find it . . ." (p. 17).

If this was Giraudoux's intention in writing *Sodome et Gomorrhe,* it is well disguised, but a rational meaning for its patently irrational conclusion can be found. The cause-and-effect relationship between the drama of the couple and the disease of empires has a parallel in the political texts which Giraudoux wrote during this period. They reveal that the lesson he drew from the events of 1940 was far from that which the critics and the press drew from his play, *Sodome et Gomorrhe.* However, it is significant that texts like *Armistice à Bordeaux, Visitations,* and *Sans Pouvoirs,* in which Giraudoux makes some frank and forthright statements about the fall of France, were not published in his lifetime, whereas the play was designed to be produced in occupied Paris with the approval of the Nazis. If it was Giraudoux's intention to repudiate publicly the mottoes and ideology of the New Order, he would have had to resort to some subterfuge to convey his message. An analysis of *Siegfried* has shown the multiplicity of associations which its characters and situations can evoke for the informed reader. Similarly, a comparison of *Sodome et Gomorrhe* with its contemporary texts throws quite a different light on the play.

The first knot to unravel is the significance of the couple. Giraudoux's almost simplistic rendering of the Bible story reduces to an absurdity Pétain's case against the average French

[13] "Appel du 20 juin 1940," *La France nouvelle,* p. 18.

citizen. Why should the marital discord of Jean and Lia lead to the destruction of Sodom and Gomorrah? There is a metaphor in *Armistice à Bordeaux* which gives a new meaning to the theme of the couple: "What I have on my arm, pulling on it, is a blind and deaf country, which follows me gropingly, and everyone seems to be like me in the street, each one stricken by a slight case of hemiplegia, engrossed, walking at a pace that is not his own, the pace of a couple, engaged in conducting through the crowd the blind and deaf country on his arm" (p. 7). What a sad metaphor, but what light it throws on the model couple, Jean and Lia, on whose unity the fate of the world seems to hang. Their quarrel is more than that of man and wife; it is a quarrel between the citizen and his country, a country that has failed him and dragged him down to defeat. There is a line from *Sodome et Gomorrhe* which suggests that the couple has a universal meaning: "Here is the human couple: a man capable of everything but who does not have his weapons; a woman who has all of them, and who, because of her childishness and madness, bruises herself to no advantage and for no glory" (p. 40). In one of the variants of the play that was stricken from the final edition there is another revealing phrase: "A perfect couple, each former member of which sold and traded himself," as well as the reply: "Don't play on words."[14] The perfect couple is, then, by Giraudoux's own admission, a play on words. The image from *Armistice à Bordeaux* shows that in the context of 1940 the couple had for Giraudoux a political connotation similar to that of "a house divided."

In *Sans Pouvoirs* the metaphor of the couple is implicit in a passage such as this: "There reigns an uneasiness, at this moment, between France and the French, which the youngest of them feel and which is not dissipated by the daily hoisting of the flag. Most of us avoid looking our country in the face for

---

[14] *Théâtre complet*, XV, 15, *Variantes*, IV.

fear of reading there, even more than a reproach of our incertitude, an admission of her weakness. . . . The war has magnified this divorce between the fate of France and the fate of the Frenchman which began in time of peace" (pp. 12–13).

Why this divorce between France and the French people? It is apparent that the word "country" and even the word "France" had taken on a different meaning for Giraudoux since the events of 1940. When he says at the end of *Armistice à Bordeaux* as he watches the exodus from Paris after the signing: "Then let us leave, too. Let us leave alone, for this blind and deaf country that each one used to have by his side, we look for it in vain. It has vanished from our hearts; it has disappeared from our arms; we shall never see it again . . . ." (p. 59), he is referring to the France of the Third Republic, the only France which he had ever known. Having spent his adult life in its service as a government functionary in the Ministry of Foreign Affairs, he knew it very well indeed; and, in his polite and hermetic manner, he had often castigated its leaders. Their ignominious collusion with the Nazis was the logical outcome of their selfish and shortsighted policies. Giraudoux remarks in that one-sided dialogue with his son which is *Armistice à Bordeaux:* "And it is true that everything happened as though our leaders, seeing defeat as a way of rescuing us, with the skill and confidence of great men, foretold it, paved the way for it, made it real" (p. 43). He goes on to say that he must now revise his last will and testament, for his son has been cheated of his inheritance. All that Giraudoux can will to him now is resentment against his elders and his leaders because of a lost war, a tarnished glory, and a vanished fatherland that can be restored to life only by a new generation (pp. 47–54).

The bitterness of Giraudoux's own resentment is reflected in *Sodome et Gomorrhe,* though here it seems to be directed against *la femme*. In *Siegfried* we have had occasion to note how the mind of this poet tended to cloak his political ideas in erotic imagery or to embody them in his fictional characters. Given Giraudoux's propensity for political symbolism, whether conscious or unconscious, it is more than likely that his mind worked in somewhat the same fashion when he was composing *Sodome et Gomorrhe*. In this irrational quarrel which he depicts between the sexes, only one thing is clear: its virulence and its inevitability. Neither sex shows any disposition to compromise in spite of the fact that the fate of the world depends on their reconciliation. But in Lia's intransigence there is a trace of madness: "You are going mad, Lia . . . and becoming cruel . . . and beastly . . . and ugly, behind your splendid face," Jean tells her (p. 45). Previously, in describing the human couple, Jean spoke of the childishness and madness of the woman, who has all the weapons, but who bruises herself to no advantage and for no glory (p. 45). In writing these lines, Giraudoux most certainly had more in mind than the battle of the sexes. This madwoman whom he describes begins to take on the features of the country that he wants to leave behind, a country where "the captain of industry is the only one who has weapons at his disposal, be they speculation or mediation."[15] This divorce between France and the French has nothing to do with *la France éternelle,* which was perhaps Giraudoux's greatest love. It is the France of the Third Republic, ruled by "the coalition of an uneasy bourgeoisie and the profiteers."[16] In the light of these parallel texts, the domestic quarrel between Jean and Lia, on whom the fate of the two cities depends, takes on a political significance. They represent the human couple not only as man and wife but also as man in relation to his society, and specifically the Frenchman in relation to the Third Republic. Their estrangement, which Giraudoux characterizes

[15] *Sans Pouvoirs,* p. 32.
[16] *Ibid.,* p. 52.

as the disease of empires, results in the end of their particular world.

This brings us to another problem of interpretation. What does Giraudoux mean by the disease of empires? The Archangel points out its symptoms: "Pleasures, recollections, objects, all take on a sex, and there are no longer any common pleasures, or a common memory, or common flowers. Evil has a sex. What that merits is the end of the world" (p. 13). This is a euphemistic diagnosis that is intelligible only to one familiar with the legend of Sodom and Gomorrah. It has its parallel, however, in a passage from *Sans Pouvoirs,* in which the reference is not to the battle of the sexes but to the class struggle. Giraudoux speaks of France as "a country where the classes, as everywhere, are divided, and where a common fate is lacking" (p. 51). "Little by little, bitterness was mounting between the classes," he noted as he recalled the events leading up to the tragedy (p. 52). This may be what he is trying to say when the Archangel is describing the uneasiness that hangs over Jean and Lia: "If for her part, it is because she is bearing a child, if for his part, it is because he is busy with his trade and imagining things, all the sins of the world can wait. But if it is because each one is stricken by the plague of Sodom, by an awareness of his own sex, then God himself won't be able to do anything about it" (p. 13). This may be an Aesopian language to describe the growing class consciousness of the French, which was reflected in the sharp cleavage between the extreme right and the extreme left. The writings of Marshal Pétain bear witness to "the violent conflicts in which the strike and the lockout vied for the honor of wreaking the greatest havoc." It was the aim of the New Order to bring about unity between what the Marshal called "capitalist feudalism" and the working class and, in his own words, "to do away with the class struggle," which the Marxists considered to be the driving force of universal progress and which Pétain maintained was an absurd concept.[17] Giraudoux seems to be denying that unity can be achieved without sacrificing one member of the couple; and sacrifice, says the Archangel, can hardly be distinguished from suicide (p. 136). The national unity which Pétain later claimed to have achieved by his revolution[18] was, according to Giraudoux, nothing more than a police state, which suppressed social conflicts by force.[19]

This does not mean that the battle of the sexes is not very real in *Sodome et Gomorrhe,* but it is not the real subject of the play, as most critics seem to think. Lia herself raises the question: "Just between you and me, it's about us, isn't it?" she asks Jean. "Isn't the end of the world merely the setting?" "One detail of the setting for the end of the couple," replies Jean enigmatically (p. 84). He seems to be generalizing the problem and implying that their quarrel is part of a much larger drama. There is nothing anywhere else in any of Giraudoux's writings to support a literal interpretation of Jean's cryptic remark. At the same time that he was writing *Sodome et Gomorrhe,* he was proposing quite the opposite end to the battle of the sexes in his one-act play, *L'Apollon de Bellac.* The only rational explanation of what the author meant by the end of the couple is a political one. André Beucler quotes Giraudoux as saying, ". . . I belong to a civilization which is crumbling, which allowed itself to be manipulated, which doubts itself; to a State which consents to being exploited by a caste."[20] Lia is identified in the author's mind with this caste or class, which had taken over the government of the Third Republic and delivered the country into the hands of the enemy. He saw the defeat of France in 1940 as just a detail in the decline and fall of bourgeois society.

[17] *La France nouvelle,* pp. 59, 60, 63, 78.
[18] *Ibid.,* pp. 81, 84.
[19] *Sans Pouvoirs,* p. 32.
[20] *Les Instants de Giraudoux,* p. 134.

Although Giraudoux owed everything he had to this society, which he had courted, espoused, and embellished, he had become thoroughly disillusioned with it. Jean awaits the Last Judgment with a certain equanimity, saying, "I no longer feel as if I am in this world which is going to end" (p. 70). In *La Folle de Chaillot* Giraudoux gave proof of his sincerity.

In the long quarrel between Jean and Lia there is no tangible reason given for their estrangement. Lia's chief complaint against Jean is his withdrawal. His physical presence is not enough to reassure her since he seems to be able to escape from her in spirit if not in body (pp. 27–28). The reason for this withdrawal can be deduced from the first scene in which Lia appears. From the very beginning she is obsessed with the idea that she is being haunted by angels. She explains that she has wrestled with them in the past but that after a violent scene they flew away and left her in peace for a time. This type of encounter is the subject of one of Giraudoux's novels, *Combat avec l'ange* (1934), in which the heroine, Maléna Paz, wrestles with the angel of jealousy. In Giraudoux's dramatic adaptation of *Tessa* (1934) the angel of domestic squabbles appears briefly on stage. But Lia points out that there is a difference between such personal demons, whose feathers she had plucked in her combat with them, and the angels who are haunting her now. The latter arrive in droves and are like "wingless ants, always on foot, tramping and pacing, and talking to one another at the crossroads like ants by means of knowing looks or facial twitches . . . talking about us" (p. 18). This is the cause of the uneasiness which hovers over their household and which the Archangel recognizes as the first symptom of what he calls the disease of empires.

Lia is obviously suffering from a kind of paranoia which has its parallel on the political plane. The key to this hermetic symbol of the haunting angels can be found in an earlier work,

Combat avec l'ange, which is a curious study of two kinds of neurasthenia (the term is Giraudoux's), jealousy and poverty. Maléna Paz, the heroine of the novel, is haunted by the fear of losing her lover, while her friend Nancy, who is very wealthy, lives in constant terror of being attacked and robbed of her possessions. The latter's neurasthenia was the effect of experiences she had during the first six years of her life, which she spent in China at the time of the Boxer Rebellion. Since then her greatest concern was to live in a safe place. "If she sold her estate at Meaux, it was because she had had enough of invasions, and not, as she put it, of hunting. If she was traveling alone in a Citroën, it was because her Rolls Royce would have made her conspicuous in Carmaux or in La Seyne, during a strike or a riot."[21] Nancy never walked through the narrow, crowded streets of the old quarters of the city, since she felt at ease only on wide avenues or near parks. Even there she dreaded finding herself face to face with one of those unfortunates who spend their lives on a park bench, which should have been reserved for children and people waiting for trolleys. Such unfortunates always sat with "their eyes staring into space, their mouths deformed by a twitch" (p. 102). One day while Maléna was curiously observing the facial expression of one of these poor wretches, that face suddenly concentrated its attention on her; and all at once she understood the fear and loathing it inspired in Nancy. That look filled her with a feeling of guilt; she was ashamed of her wealth, her jewels, her fine clothes, as if her neighbor's poverty were her own fault and not a kind of neurasthenia, as she had been accustomed to thinking (p. 105). Nancy and Maléna doubtless have the same mentality as that of the multimillionairesses who idolized Dumas because he worked his way from poverty to become the manager of a big steel company, thus proving that the poor do not have to remain

[21] *Combat avec l'ange* (Paris: Grasset, 1934), pp. 81–82.

poor and absolving the rich of the responsibility of sharing their unearned wealth.[22] This deeply rooted fear of the underprivileged classes which Giraudoux portrayed in Nancy and Maléna would seem to explain the strange obsession of Lia, who is ready to sacrifice everything to see "the little wingless angels run in the face of pitch and oil" (p. 104). In trying to reason with Lia and persuade her to make her peace with Jean in order to save Sodom and Gomorrah, the Angel (this one is not an hallucination but a messenger of God in keeping with the Biblical text) becomes exasperated with Lia's intransigence and warns her bluntly, "All these men and women whom you hate are going to multiply profusely" (p. 94).

The flight of "the little wingless angels in the face of pitch and oil" must have evoked for the spectator of 1943 the exodus of 1940 when thousands of French families fled to the south of France to escape the onslaught of the German tanks. While Lia watched the spectacle with glee, Jean looked with deep sympathy on the stricken people who were fleeing from Sodom: "Come and see human beings at the height of their intelligence, which is fear; at the height of their generosity, which is flight . . . " (p. 65). This paradoxical allusion to the exodus of 1940 troubled many a critic who was not sure whether the author was being ironic or sincere. The ambiguity was probably intentional, given the historical moment, but any doubt as to the author's true sentiments can be dispelled by a cross-reference to *Sans Pouvoirs*. The exodus of 1940 was "the foremost of our crimes, according to our interpreters," said Giraudoux, who undertook to defend it as follows: "France was then stirred by one of the most beautiful movements that Europe has ever known. It was the exodus. . . . An entire people, known and often mocked for their attachment to a patch of land, a routine existence, and physical comforts, renounced their soil, their dwell-

[22] See p. 39.

ings, the necessities of life, to reach a holy place—which was the free country. There were thousands in flight, thousands who were afraid . . . " (pp. 24–25).

The divergent opinions of Jean and Lia are reflected in their quarrel over the weather. Weather is the theme of the first scene between Jean and Lia, and it is repeated in the final scene of the play. In the beginning, Jean remarks on what a beautiful day it is, but Lia immediately takes the opposite viewpoint and eventually calls upon the Angel to rule on the question of whether the sun is shining or whether a storm is brewing. Oddly enough, the Angel agrees with Lia, maintaining that Lia is right and that Jean is blind. The Angel warns that a note of death has slipped into every song and that the end of the world is near. In the final scene when the wrath of God is about to strike, Lia again starts an argument about the weather, reminding Jean that she was right the first time. Jean stoutly maintains that the weather was magnificent the other day but that today is the most sinister of his whole life. Lia, contrary to the end, insists that it is now the most beautiful day of her life, that there is not a cloud in the sky, that the sun is brightly shining; in short, that it is an ideal end of the world. Even after the darkness descends and all are struck down, the voices of Jean and Lia are heard, still at odds:

JEAN. Forgive us, Heaven! What a night!
LIA. Thank you, Heaven! What a dawn!

This apparently senseless quarrel over the weather makes a good deal of sense if interpreted in a political context. The social reforms of the Popular Front Government directly preceding the Munich Pact created a political climate which was good for the average French citizen like Jean, but to the hard core of French reactionaries who had never even accepted the French Revolution, it seemed like the beginning of the end.

Rather than submit to mass rule, many of them looked to
Hitler as the strong man of the hour. In the end of the Third
Republic they saw a deliverance and the dawn of a New Order,
even at the price of invasion and defeat. Lia represents this
extreme right-wing group, which was more afraid of its own
people than of the Nazis.[23] It is significant that when the end
comes and the two sexes separate to receive the celestial punishment, Lia is the only one who is not afraid:

> JACQUES. Are all you women afraid?
> LIA. Why, all? Here there is but one woman. The only woman.
> JEAN. So much the worse for you. Here we are thousands, millions
> of men. (p. 108)

Alone in her exultant madness, Lia is more readily identified
with the minority of Frenchmen who welcomed Hitler than
she is with the other members of her sex. The irreconcilable
quarrel between Jean and Lia while the end of the world is
threatening is a transparent symbol of the struggle between the
ruling class, *la patrie* of *Armistice à Bordeaux,* and the average
French citizen of *Sans Pouvoirs.* To the Anglo-Saxon reader,
who is more familiar with the legend of Sodom and Gomorrah
than with the linguistic practice of classifying nouns by gender,
the segregation of the sexes tends to have only one association.
For the Frenchman, *la femme* in this particular context can
evoke a number of feminine nouns: *la patrie, la France, la*

[23] For Marshal Pétain's reaction to the social laws, see *La France
nouvelle,* p. 60. An article in the *New York Times* magazine section
of November 7, 1965, "The French Revolution Has Been Lost," by Jean-
François Revel, points out the deep cleavage between the right and the
left in France before World War II: "Few foreigners can imagine the
hatred of the French ruling classes for Léon Blum's modest reforms at the
time of the Popular Front [vacations with pay, social security, workers'
pensions]. The enthusiastic welcome these extreme reactionaries gave to
Marshal Pétain—and even to France's defeat, which killed the Republic—
can be explained only in this way" (p. 29).

République, la bourgeoisie, not to mention *Marianne,* the personification of the French Republic. The contest between *la femme* and millions of Frenchmen was bound to have political overtones for the public of 1943, in spite of the Biblical framework of the play. As darkness descended on Lia's dawn, many a Parisian in the audience who had welcomed the dawn of the New Order must have felt the point of the author's satire after three years of Nazi occupation.

Lia does not have the last word, however. Though everything is in ashes, the angry voices are still heard, as Giraudoux affirms with splendid irony:

> THE ARCHANGEL. Are they never going to be quiet! Are they never going to die?
> THE ANGEL. They are dead.
> THE ARCHANGEL. Then who is speaking?
> THE ANGEL. They are. Death was not enough. The scene continues.

France has lost a battle, but not the war. The fight goes on. The end of this particular world does not mean the end of the class struggle nor even of the battle of the sexes.

The critics gave *Sodome et Gomorrhe* a chilly reception. Some saw more Voltaire than Racine in the play.[24] Others accused Giraudoux of taking himself too seriously or even of parodying his own work.[25] The reaction seems to have been one of general stupefaction, either because of the bitterness with which Giraudoux depicted the marital conflict or because of the double meaning that was unmentionable at the time. Despite the coldness of the press, the play enjoyed a great success. The number of performances reached the very respectable figure of 214, only

[24] Jean Silvain in *Appel,* October 21, 1943, and L. Cheronnet in *Le Théâtre,* October 30, 1943.
[25] Alain Laubreaux in *Je suis partout,* October 15, 1943.

40 less than that of *Amphitryon 38*.[26] It was not until the author's death four months after the opening of the play (Giraudoux died on January 31, 1944) that the collaborationist newspapers admitted that they had been taken. The following comment appeared in *Je suis partout,* a notorious organ of the Nazis and the collaborators:

> Jean Giraudoux must not die. Seriously, now. This is neither the time, nor the place. Or in any case, not in that way. To do it properly, since there is still time, let *Sodome et Gomorrhe* be withdrawn from that barren sugar-loaf, the Théatre Hébertot, and be replaced by *Electre*. Let M. Marcel Bertrand be driven out of the Opéra-Comique. Let the last copies of *Choix des élues* be reduced to pulp. We must organize the defense of the real Giraudoux.[27]

Fortunately, there is no need to defend Giraudoux from the image of him that these gentlemen would like to have projected. Giraudoux's writings speak for themselves, if one can study

[26] Information furnished by the Théâtre Hébertot and the Théâtre de l'Athénée. See Appendix II.

[27] The Nazis were misled by Giraudoux's *Siegfried* into thinking that he was a Germanophile. They liked his play *Electre* because they saw in it an apology for dictatorship. They were somewhat less enthusiastic about *Amphitryon 38* and *La Guerre de Troie n'aura pas lieu* because both plays are antiwar. Marcel Bertrand's opera based on *Amphitryon 38* was playing at the Opéra-Comique concurrently with *Sodome et Gomorrhe*. *Choix des élues* is a novel which Giraudoux published in 1939. I do not know why the Nazis took exception to it. The article quoted above appeared on February 4, 1944. On February 11, 1944, *Je suis partout* printed the following letter to the editor from Céline, a well-known novelist before the war, who collaborated quite openly with the Nazis: "On the q.t., the Jews must be splitting their sides reading Giraudoux's obituary notices! A way of kissing their ass indirectly. We know what we mean . . . in the name of *belles lettres* . . . of French thought and so forth! Get out the brush and the whitewash! Suppose I drop dead or that someone kills me, I should like to see the Izvestias scribbling out my obituary notices! Ah! Just a minute! Every day I regret being an Aryan . . . !"

his work as a whole, but there is a tendency in academic circles to ignore Giraudoux's last works or to dismiss them as decadent. Nothing is more regrettable. It was during the Occupation that Giraudoux spoke his mind. His suppressed desire for revolt is reflected in Jean's remark to Lia: "For five years you have lived with a man whom you thought the most malleable, the most courteous, and the calmest of creatures. He is in fact headstrong, insolent, and wildly unrestrained . . ." (pp. 102–103). This admission should warn us to look beneath the polite façade of his fictional characters, whose scintillating dialogue does not always reveal the depth of emotion from which it stems.

When Giraudoux died, leaving *Sodome et Gomorrhe* as his last testament, so to speak, many felt at the time that he took with him the key to a baffling universe that they would never succeed in penetrating. Of all Giraudoux's plays, this is the most puzzling and the least appealing, but it was not meant to please. It is the direct product of a time of crisis, which demands something other than masterpieces of its writers. At least this is the opinion which Giraudoux expressed after the troubled days of 1934, which were a sinister prelude to the collapse of 1940. In an article he wrote on the subject of the author as journalist, he stated:

> What the readers of 1935 are asking for is precisely the contrary of what their fathers demanded. They no longer ask for masterpieces; nor do they require the constant literary purring which is the echo of happy and bourgeois eras; they ask for a sensibility and a vocabulary. . . . In other words, the writer should become, in the work of his century, an element that is always mobilizable each day, an all-day worker, a day laborer, or *journalier*—that is to say, a journalist.[28]

[28] "L'Ecrivain journaliste," *Marianne*, February 14, 1934. This was published after the fascist riot of February 6, which also occasioned the publication of the original version of the final act of *Siegfried*, prophesying the violent death of the German Republic.

Giraudoux meant what he said, for like the gardener in *Visitations,* he was an indefatigable commentator on current events. Not only did he write newspaper articles and deliver public lectures, but most of his plays and his novels reflect his preoccupation with the major issues of the day. There were moments when Giraudoux prudently avoided attacking a subject which might have political overtones. *Tessa* (1934) and *Ondine* (1939) are pure escapism and could not by any stretch of the imagination be identified with the crises that preceded them. But such is not the case with *Sodome et Gomorrhe.* It is certainly no masterpiece, but neither is it an evasion of controversial questions.

During the dark days of the Occupation, Giraudoux could have remained silent like Racine when his security was threatened; or he could have gone underground and published clandestinely under an assumed name, as did other writers of the Resistance. But some inner compulsion, perhaps the need for public confession, forced him to speak his mind through his chosen medium, the theater. "Eras are not at peace with themselves unless to those radiant confessionals which are the theatres and the arenas the crowd comes, and as far as possible, in its most striking confessional dress, to increase the solemnity and to listen to its own confessions of cowardice and sacrifice, hate and passion," he says in *Visitations* (pp. 127–128). Giraudoux wrote *Sodome et Gomorrhe* as a reply to Pétain and placed the blame for the defeat squarely where he felt it belonged, on the class which preferred the intervention of a foreign power to compromise with a democratic opposition. Though his message is sardonically disguised as a quarrel between man and wife in a Biblical setting, this Aesopian presentation, further obscured by the author's famous preciosity, enabled Giraudoux to deliver it publicly before the very people who he felt were responsible for the defeat. Having thus relieved his conscience, Giraudoux went on to prescribe a drastic remedy for the "disease of empires" in a play which he timed for the liberation but which he did not live to see produced, *The Madwoman of Chaillot.*

✧ VI ✧

La Folle de Chaillot

La Folle de Chaillot was produced posthumously, but it is not an unfinished work, such as *Sans Pouvoirs*. On the contrary, it was of all Jean Giraudoux's plays the most carefully written and the most frequently reworked since *Siegfried,* his first theatrical endeavor. We have, on that score, Louis Jouvet's testimony:

> In the sequence of his works, *La Folle de Chaillot* will no doubt be in a place "by itself," and will most certainly give those who have talked so much about Giraudoux's *"préciosité"* an opportunity to evaluate their own judgment. Different, indeed, from all his other plays, for some, perhaps, it will be a true revelation. Let those people in particular take note that we shall begin rehearsals immediately and that we shall perform it tomorrow, in accordance with the final proofs, based on four successive copies, revised and corrected by the author. . . .[1]

Why did Jouvet put such sharp and precise emphasis on the fact that *La Folle de Chaillot* was a finished work? One look at the subject of the play is enough to explain why it was likely to shock many enthusiasts of Giraudoux's theatre. The setting is the sidewalk of the Café Chez Francis, where three shady characters are in the process of founding a corporation for the pur-

---

[1] *Opéra,* December 12, 1945. The play opened December 19, 1945, at the Théâtre de l'Athénée.

pose of prospecting the subsoil of Paris. An old woman who frequents the district discovers the conspiracy and restores to life a handsome young man who almost died in that venture; then she takes it upon herself to set a trap for the profiteers, has them condemned to death by a people's tribunal, and imprisons them forever in the underground they had planned to prospect. Thus, by the prompt and decisive action of the Madwoman of Chaillot, Paris is freed from the forces of evil and restored to youth and happiness.

Needless to say, not everyone was pleased to see the author of *Electre* cast off his cloak of ambiguity and recommend such an unequivocal solution to the problems of Free France. Despite the words of Louis Jouvet, it was rumored that Giraudoux had not really written *La Folle de Chaillot* or that the play was not in finished form,[2] but the exaltation of the historical moment, the glory that surrounded the author's name, and the emotion so many felt upon hearing the dead poet's last message prevailed over the insinuations of hostile critics. The play enjoyed a long run in Paris, and two years later, in the English adaptation by Maurice Valency,[3] it was the first of Giraudoux's plays to become a Broadway hit.[4] Since then *The Madwoman of Chaillot* has been a popular offering by summer stock companies and amateur theatrical groups. In fact, the vogue which Giraudoux's theater has been enjoying in the United States seems to have been launched by the success of this particular work. In spite of its open indictment of big business as the chief cause of war and suffering, *The Madwoman of Chaillot*, like Beaumarchais'

[2] Roger Gabert, "Aux feux de la Critique," in the edition of *La Folle de Chaillot* published by *Le Monde illustré, théatral et littéraire*, July 4 and 5, 1947. See also the article by Léon Treich, in *L'Ordre*, December 21, 1945, and in *Mondes*, December 26, 1945.

[3] New York: Random House, 1947.

[4] *La Folle de Chaillot* ran for 297 performances in Paris and 368 in New York.

Marriage of Figaro, had the distinction of being applauded by the very powers which it attacked. The critics who liked the play passed off its revolutionary message as intellectual spoofing; the few who were suspicious of the author's intentions labeled the *Madwoman* a work of decadence.

The artistic and entertainment value of the play has withstood the test of time, but unlike Beaumarchais' masterpiece, *La Folle de Chaillot* has never been taken seriously as a work of propaganda, partly because such a possibility seemed so little in keeping with the image of the urbane and witty diplomat which Giraudoux had carefully fostered in his prewar works. However, the bitter and quarrelsome tone of *Sodome et Gomorrhe* revealed a Giraudoux on the verge of revolt and waiting for the moment when he could attack openly those whom he held responsible for the defeat of 1940. A study of the genesis of *La Folle de Chaillot* may show that it deserves to rank with *Le Mariage de Figaro* as a rare combination of good theatre and militant literature.

The play was conceived in 1942 at the same time as *Sodome et Gomorrhe,*[5] but the final version dates from 1943, according to Pierre Lestringuez:

> One day, at the Hotel de Castille, around the end of December 1943, when he had only one month to live, I went to pick up Jean Giraudoux for lunch and found him seated at the small table, so awkward for writing, which he used as a desk. I apologized for disturbing him at his work. "Not at all," he said. "I'm not working, I'm prophesying." And on the manuscript of *La Folle de Chaillot* he showed me the words he had just written by way of an epigraph: "This play was first produced by the Louis Jouvet company, at the Théâtre de l'Athénée, on October 17, 1945."[6]

[5] See the program of *L'Apollon de Bellac* and *Visitations.*
[6] *XXᵉ Siècle,* December 13, 1945.

The projected date of the performance was Pierre Lestringuez's birthday, as the latter explained in another interview.[7]

The bond between Pierre Lestringuez and Jean Giraudoux was more than that of friendship. It was also the tie that binds soldiers who have fought side by side. However, veterans though they were of World War I, the battle they fought together followed close on the heels of the Munich Pact, and the battlefield was the stage of the first theatre of the Republic. On October 13, 1938, Lestringuez's play *Tricolore* opened at the Comédie Française, co-billed with a one-act play by Jean Giraudoux, *Cantiques des Cantiques,* written especially for the occasion.[8] The critics found Giraudoux's offering innocuous enough, but they raised quite a furor over *Tricolore* because, as the title indicates, it evoked memories of the French Revolution. The heroine of the play is Théroigne de Méricourt, whom the author described as "a great courtesan, perhaps, but also one of the most engaging and curious characters of the French Revolution, for she was one of the first feminists."[9] Other plays on similar subjects had done well a year or two before,[10] but after the Munich Pact of 1938 the political climate was unfavorable to staging a play about the French Revolution. The press opened fire the day after the dress rehearsal. "It is a mistake, a rather crude mistake which must be quickly forgotten," declared one right-wing newspaper.[11] After the first-night performance, another reactionary news sheet stated bluntly, "This is not the time to flaunt on stage memories of a period when the French people were divided against each other or to magnify the stocking-knitters with their

[7] *Nouvelles du Matin*, December 18, 1945.

[8] Interview with J. Giraudoux, in *Le Figaro,* October 11, 1938.

[9] Interview with Pierre Lestringuez, in *Ce Soir,* April 6, 1938.

[10] *Mme. Capet* and *Mme. Quinze,* according to Pierre Lièvre, in *Le Mercure de France,* November 15, 1938.

[11] *L'Ordre,* October 13, 1938.

plumes and sabers."[12] *Le Figaro, Le Temps, Le Journal,* and *L'Oeuvre* all joined in the chorus. The press was particularly disturbed because the play gave every indication of being a popular success.[13] Two days after it opened, *L'Ordre,* which had spearheaded the attack, reproduced a hair-raising portrait of the real Théroigne de Méricourt as she looked the year before she died, raving mad, in prison. This was intended to remind the public of the horrible fate of "the Amazon of freedom," as she was called, and to counterbalance the startling chic of the actress who played the leading role. The harsh judgment of the press, however, was not enough to keep the spectators away from the box office. Meanwhile, the author had been mobilized for another war and was comfortably sitting out the siege of his play at Besançon, where he had been called up by the government. From here he wrote to André Warnod of *Le Figaro:* "Wish me luck and give me news of the battle of *Tricolore* here in the peaceful garrison where I am stationed." After sixty-eight performances the play finally had to be withdrawn because of the noisy demonstrations that drowned out the performers. Jean Giraudoux indignantly withdrew his play, *Cantique des Cantiques,* and refused to allow the Comédie Française to revive it without *Tricolore.*[14] The story of that battle, which began in October, 1938, explains in part Giraudoux's mysterious prediction that *La Folle de Chaillot* would be performed for the first time on October 17, 1945. The month of October marked more than one anniversary. Not only was it Pierre Lestringuez's birthday but Giraudoux's as well, for he was born on October 29, 1882. But most of all, his dedication recalled the creation of *Tricolore* and the re-creation of that madwoman of the French Revolution, Théroigne de Méricourt.

[12] *Le Petit Bleu,* October 14, 1938.
[13] Pierre Lièvre, in *Echo de Paris,* October 21, 1938.
[14] I received this information from Pierre Lestringuez himself.

Sodome et Gomorrhe is a play of the defeat, written for occupied France. *La Folle de Chaillot* is a play of revolution, written for free men. One may wonder why Giraudoux never wrote a play about the liberation. In *Sodome et Gomorrhe* he implied that the defeat was only a detail of a universal drama, which was class warfare. Similarly, he saw the liberation of France from the German occupation as a mere detail of the real struggle that lay ahead, which must be a revolution to rid France of the profiteers. He was already thinking of postwar France and the future of the world:

> Whether it be in the name of faith, of wisdom, or of the desire for earthly comfort, one can only tremble at the idea of that future, for it is vain to hope for the peace or happiness of that humanity whose actions will be prompted everywhere by the same wrath of banks, publicity, and law, that humanity whose every tribe, as it comes to have less and less reason to distinguish itself from the others, will gather, with increasing scorn, under a totem of pride and war which will be the nation. Such is the danger that is now threatening all civilizations, and not only our own.[15]

Always on the alert to warn the French people against their old enemy, war, in *La Folle de Chaillot* he gets down to the root of the problem and presents what he considers to be the only effective preventative: revolution.

As a matter of fact, during the Occupation everyone was talking revolution, and most of all the Vichy government.[16] The word which was unmentionable in 1938 was now blazoned all over the newspapers. But the revolution that was being advocated so openly in 1943 with the blessing of the Nazis was not the one that most Frenchmen had in mind, and certainly not Jean Giraudoux, as we shall see in *La Folle de Chaillot*.

[15] *Sans Pouvoirs,* p. 146.
[16] See Marshal Pétain's speeches.

With his usual clairvoyance, Giraudoux calculated that the liberation would come to pass during the spring or summer of 1945, that Jouvet would return to France, and that his play could be produced in the fall of that year. His first two suppositions were correct: the Germans surrendered on May 8, 1945, and Jouvet returned from his exile in South America, but he was two months behind Giraudoux's timetable in producing the play. *La Folle de Chaillot* had its première on December 19, 1945, just in time to give Paris a sparkling Christmas entertainment and a significant message for the New Year. Giraudoux's play was the crowning triumph of the liberation and a great social and political event. As a matter of fact, it was thanks to the government, and in particular to Jacques Joujard, director general of Arts and Letters, that Jouvet's theatre received the subsidy needed for a production worthy of the play. The first-night performance was given for the benefit of the Association des Résistants de 1940, with General de Gaulle in the audience, while André Malraux, the new minister of Information, attended the dress rehearsal.[17] The elite of Paris came to pay homage to the dead poet and to receive his last message.

If Giraudoux foresaw the date when his play could be performed, he also foresaw that the time would come when he might venture to speak his mind. Not too openly, however, for he knew that he would be addressing the same public as before— a public less powerful and less sure of itself, it is true, but one that thought only of returning to prewar days. He knew that most of his audience would be opposed to the task he meant to propose and that the remedy he prescribed would have to be skillfully concocted so as to produce the greatest and the most lasting effect. Giraudoux was still mindful of the words of Jouvet: "No dramatic work is valid if it does not find an audience

17 *Opéra,* December 12, 1945, testimony of Louis Jouvet.

to listen to it and to make it live."[18] A play that fails is of little use, for even though it creates a brief scandal, it never reaches the public for which it was intended. The lesson of *Tricolore* was not lost on Giraudoux: revolution is a subject the dramatist broaches at great risk, whether he is evoking the past or militating for the future. Besides, *Tricolore* was not Giraudoux's first experience with a cabal. His *Judith* (1931) had been a victim of the same critics and the same newspapers that killed *Tricolore*. True, their attack was milder, but it was no less effective, for *Judith* was withdrawn like *Tricolore*—at the height of its success and at the end of sixty-one performances, for reasons that had nothing to do with the merit of the play.[19] It is, therefore, to be expected that Giraudoux would try to make his message as palatable as possible so that *La Folle de Chaillot* would not suffer the same fate as *Tricolore*.

The first lesson that Giraudoux learned from *Tricolore* and *Judith* was not to embody his criticism of society in the personage of a chic young girl. Such a play to the gallery invariably alarmed the critics. The fact that one newspaper found it expedient to publish the portrait of Théroigne de Méricourt in the guise of a madwoman may have given Giraudoux his cue to personify the spirit of revolution in the person of an eccentric old lady who was a familiar figure in certain quarters of Paris. Giraudoux rightly guessed that the spectators and the critics would be more interested in discovering the biographical key to

[18] *Réflexions du comédien* (Paris: Nouvelle Revue Critique, 1938), p. 42.

[19] See *Comoedia,* December 14, 1931: "M. Jean Giraudoux's play *Judith* has been temporarily removed from the marquee of the Théâtre Pigalle, at the very moment when the extremely brilliant receipts assured the work a long and fruitful run. Indeed, we may add that the day before yesterday the Théâtre Pigalle had to turn people away." The only explanation given in the article was that the play had been withdrawn owing to previous obligations to Jules Romains for his play *Le Roi Masqué,* with the comment that the latter categorically denied this.

his heroine than in discussing the idea which she represented. As a matter of fact, several newspapers printed descriptions of the individual who served as model for the role:

> Every evening around seven, before the war, the customers of "Chez Francis," the well-known corner café on the Place de l'Alma, whose customers—among whom one often found Jean Giraudoux—would see emerge from the Avenue George V an astounding creature. Augustin, the bartender, would stop shaking his cocktails, and the old organ-grinder from the bridge, with his metal leg, his hook arm, and his cap with a leather visor, would say: "Well, it's seven o'clock; there's the Madwoman of Chaillot. Hello, Môme Bijoux." And Jean Giraudoux would smile at the apparition. Every evening at seven, she was the "Madwoman of Chaillot." At midnight, in the Rue Fromentin or in the Avenue Rachel, creating around her in the Rue Pigalle a circle of uneasy curiosity, she became the "Môme Bijoux." Under a hat of faded feathers would appear her plaster-white face, spotted with black. . . . She never spoke to anyone.[20]

André Beucler in *Les Instants de Giraudoux* recalls a conversation that the two men had one evening in 1939 as they were strolling through the Clichy district, a favorite haunt of "la Môme Bijoux." They happened to pass by the Théâtre Pigalle, which reminded them of Giraudoux's unhappy experience with *Judith* in 1931. His unorthodox version of the murder of Holophernes by the beautiful Jewess was a tragedy in more ways than one after the brilliant success of *Siegfried* and *Amphitryon 38*. The memory of some of the critics' cruel remarks still rankled, as is shown in the following words of Giraudoux reported by Beucler:

> I no longer think about the beautiful virgin of Israel, in love and complicated, who was so abashed by her sacrifice that she fell a victim to femininity at the very peak of pride and was furious

[20] *Paris Soir,* August 30, 1945.

at being led by a prophecy, and who ended by killing a male, as one kills in Montmartre. Or rather, if I still think of that "embethuliating" play[21] . . . it's because I have just had the idea of a supplement, yes: *Judith, or the Danger of Missions!* (p. 33)

Meanwhile, the two men entered a café and sat down at a table facing the madwoman of Clichy, whom Giraudoux observed musingly:

However, our neighbor also opens up new horizons for me. She is not like Electre; she makes no sign to the gods, for she does not wish to bring down their wrath on mankind. She is satisfied to confound them—she's mad . . . that's just what I mean—mad, from seeing men bungle their lives and throw everything into confusion. But not all of them, actually. She has allies, subjects. She is no doubt inaccessible. But she has one passion. She is the enemy of the abstract, speculating breed, makers of all manner of corporations in the sense that we say "maker of angels."[22] She is a living indictment, a revenge that is brewing, the embodiment of disdain. She knows the paths of wisdom and her eye is a conspiracy. But also a salvation. We must propagate her sensibility. (p. 34)

One may have doubts about the authenticity of conversations reported from memory, but this one reveals a train of thought which is paralleled in Giraudoux's writings. His approach to social change was not that of the parliamentarian who works through the slow and cumbersome machinery of the democratic process. Giraudoux had little confidence in the efficacy of parliamentary government. He was more inclined to what he called the feminine approach to politics. In a series of lectures on the Frenchwoman and France, he characterized the opposite sex thus:

[21] Word invented by one of the critics to express his annoyance with *Judith*. The word is derived from Béthulie, the name of Judith's country.
[22] That is, an abortionist.

Woman lives in the present; she has a taste for quick solutions and immediate retribution. The natural horror she has of suffering and injustice leads her to meet daily problems with quick solutions, even temporary or partial ones, rather than put her trust in political action, which is so slow and so questionable, whatever its range....[23]

This passage goes back to 1934, but it so sharply recalls the first paragraph of his chapter on the future of France in *Sans Pouvoirs* that it shows Giraudoux to be very obviously an advocate of what he calls feminine methods of action: "This, then, is the Frenchman's duty. He is not to call upon France for help this time; he is to come to hers. There is nothing to do but run, as if to a fire. No long preparation; that is merely lost time; straight to the problem" (p. 125). Here Giraudoux expresses all the impetuosity of youth, although he attributes it to femininity: "Whereas man, as in France, in 1789, or like the Russians, in 1917, took a hundred years of conservation and preparation to start revolutions, women, who did not understand change until July 14, at twelve noon, immediately joined in on July 14, at quarter past twelve, not because they understood the reforms that revolution works toward, but because they understood the spirit of revolution" (p. 173).

These are the ideas that must have been in the back of his mind as he observed "la Môme Bijoux" that night when he was chatting with André Beucler. The vision of the madwoman was to haunt him during the grim years that followed. Giraudoux alluded to her again in *Visitations,* the lecture he gave in Switzerland in 1942. Among the characters and themes which peopled his imagination and which he describes in this lecture is the vision of a young attaché wearing a morning coat and spectacles, his hair slicked down with brilliantine. He is receiving a former

[23] *La Française et la France* (Paris: Gallimard, 1951), p. 134.

President, who had governed France and Europe for ten years and who is waiting to see the current President. The attaché, dazzled by this *tête à tête* with a great man, addresses the former President as follows: "I arrive, and my first day on the job, instead of giving subsidies to a journalist or showing out the madwoman who comes every morning to advise the President, my first assignment is to receive you, to see you" (p. 77). Full of candor and sincere admiration, he seizes the opportunity to ask the former President a question that has been bothering him for a long time: "What is the secret of politics, Mr. President? What is the secret of wisdom? For I persist in thinking that they are only one side of the same vocation" (p. 78). This recalls the conversation quoted by Beucler in which Giraudoux noted that the madwoman knew the paths of wisdom. The former President evades the naive question of the attaché, who is quick to realize that he has been indiscreet. Their *tête à tête* is interrupted by the daily visit of the madwoman, whom the former President does not recognize. "In my time the one who used to come was a wise woman. That didn't work any better. . . . I leave you with the madwoman. . . . Listen well to what she has to say" (p. 82). Whereupon he goes into the President's office while the attaché, flushed and abashed, receives the madwoman.

This little scene resembles a dream sequence in which elements are derived from real life but from different times and places. The young attaché is the author himself, who entered the Ministry of Foreign Affairs in 1910 and was promoted to the rank of attaché in 1912. As Giraudoux explains in *Visitations,* the memory of that youth "still adolescent and unsophisticated, beginning his career under the most corrupt old men and in the most terrible situations" (p. 77), is one of the visions that has been haunting him. The former President was doubtless Clemenceau and the incumbent, Raymond Poincaré, who alternated in the post of prime minister (Président du Conseil)[24] during the early years of Giraudoux's career. The identity of the madwoman is obvious enough though her presence in this particular context is more than a little puzzling. Fortunately, there is an account by another witness which suggests more specifically the association which the madwoman may have had for Giraudoux in this scene. The witness is Louis Aragon, who also relates a conversation he had with Jean Giraudoux in the fall of 1939. The latter, in his capacity of Commissioner General of Information, had summoned Aragon, who was the leading representative of the Communist press, to warn him that the government was about to suspend publication of *Ce Soir* and *L'Humanité*. Aragon gave the following account of that interview in an homage to Giraudoux published in October 1944:

> Then Giraudoux came in. He was a man who was beside himself; it was clear that he was already right in the midst of that undeclared war; it was clear that he no longer spoke in his own name, that he was caught up in a destiny that was not his own, that he was the toy of an Aeschylean fatality. He knew already that I disapproved of that frightful venture [the war] we were involved in, that I found the methods adopted in the Rue de Grenelle and the Rue Saint Dominique [the War Offices] quite mad; he did not disapprove of me; he understood me; he told me so; he did not question my reasons for objecting so strongly to that which, in fact, we were then forbidden to question; he told me that he believed in my patriotism; he told me. . . .[25]

One can guess how the vision of the madwoman, who came daily to the President's office to offer her advice, represents the radical press, disguised as *la Môme Bijoux*. The fact that the

[24] Clemenceau was Prime Minister from 1906–1909 just before Giraudoux entered the diplomatic service. Poincaré was Prime Minister in 1912, the year Giraudoux was promoted to attaché.

[25] "Jean Giraudoux et l'Achéron," *Confluences*, XXXV, 128.

French government and the French Communists each thought the other equally mad should not confuse the reader. Lia's madness is that of the extreme right, which Jean could no longer tolerate. The madness of Aurélie, the Madwoman of Chaillot, is an Aristophanic mask for the madness of the extreme left, which Giraudoux was beginning to consider more akin to political wisdom. As one critic observed: "Wisdom since Aristophanes has always been expressed through the mouths of madmen, whose feigned foolishness tempered the bitterness of their remarks. Aurélie alone was able to put across lines that probably startled, and indeed shocked, the audience. Thus the serene improbability of the plot gave the heroine's fundamental truths that support without which *La Folle de Chaillot* would have been no more than a savage pamphlet."[26]

Such is the association of ideas that led Giraudoux to embody his theme of social revolution in the unlikely person of a madwoman. The mad heroine of *Tricolore* doubtless gave him the initial idea, which was crystallized by the encounter with *la Môme Bijoux* on that evening described by André Beucler. The political background of this crystallization can be inferred from the interview with Louis Aragon and the allusion to the madwoman in the scene from *Visitations*. Finally, madness was a convenient mask which made it possible for Giraudoux to convey his message without offending his audience. Thus it is that "the revolution which has epithets but no date"[27] is personified by the Madwoman of Chaillot.

The setting which Giraudoux chose for the first act of his fantasy is the sidewalk café Chez Francis, which is situated in a fashionable quarter of Paris frequented by tourists, well-to-do bourgeois, and government functionaries like the author. The Café Francis in the Place de l'Alma is on the right bank of the

[26] Pol Gaillard, *Les Lettres françaises,* December 28, 1945.
[27] *Pour une politique urbaine,* p. 115.

Seine, facing the Eiffel Tower on the right and on the left the Quai d'Orsay, where Giraudoux lived and worked. In an early version of the play, there is a plot to bomb the Eiffel Tower, but in the final version the target is changed to the home of the villain's adversary, identified by the initiated with Giraudoux's apartment house, which is also visible from the sidewalk of the Café Francis.

Such bourgeois surroundings would hardly seem an appropriate setting for a proletarian revolution unless one bears in mind that this one is a fantasy emerging from the brain of a bourgeois writer and destined for a bourgeois audience. Viewed in this light, Giraudoux's treatment of his subject is quite in keeping with the bourgeois concept that revolutions stem from an idea or a conspiracy rather than from a social and economic phenomenon. Louis Dumur's well-known novel *Les Défaitistes* (1923) popularized the belief that the Russian revolution was cradled in the Café de la Rotonde by Trotsky and a group of left-wing journalists. Zelten, the eccentric revolutionary of *Siegfried et le Limousin,* also frequented La Rotonde. In fact, the café was the natural habitat of revolutionaries and intellectuals. Literary as well as social revolutions emanated from it. There is even a legend, exploited by Giraudoux in a variant of the final scene of the first act, that Nicolas Boileau, Molière, Jean Racine, and Jean de la Fontaine used to meet in a café in the same location as the Café Francis to discuss their works and to lay down guidelines for French classicism.

The Café Francis evoked for the Parisian of the 1940's a host of associations more appropriate to the author and his subject than the Place de la Bastille, the usual rallying ground for revolutionary movements. Even the proletariat is not lacking in this setting—not the factory worker, of course, but the waiters, the dishwashers, the flower girls, the shoelace vendors, the ragpicker, the sewerman, in short all those unfortunates who live on the crumbs that fall from the tables of the rich and the only kind of proletariat that the bourgeois writer or spectator is likely to be familiar with. After all, is not the relationship between the waiter and the customer a symbolic representation of the class structure of bourgeois society?

Giraudoux remarked jokingly in a variant of *Cantique des Cantiques* that for many years he had felt the urge to clear up two misunderstandings: that of the waiter and the customer, and that of France and Germany.[28] Giraudoux attacked both these subjects in *Siegfried,* but only the latter was clearly recognizable at the time. In the following decade the problem of class conflict loomed even larger on the horizon than the Franco-German problem. The former is treated symbolically in *Cantique des Cantiques,* the one-act play which Giraudoux wrote as a curtain raiser for *Tricolore.* The scene is a café; the characters are two men and a woman. On the surface the plot seems to be nothing more than the eternal triangle. The woman, Florence, is in the process of breaking off with her rich lover, the President, Claude. (Giraudoux's plays are peopled with presidents, either of corporations or political bodies. He rarely bothers to differentiate between them, considering, no doubt, that their power all stems from the same source, money.) In spite of his generosity towards her, Claude overwhelms her by the grandeur of his preoccupations: "With you, I was conscious only of the great professions, the great enterprises. I was aware of and followed the struggles of the world, its thirsts and its treasures. With you it was oil, gold, iron. . . ."[29] She could have added "war," but several days before the play opened Daladier had just signed the Munich Pact, which was supposed to assure peace in our time. In prefer-

---

[28] *Théâtre Complet,* XIV, *Variantes,* III, 82.
[29] *Théâtre complet,* VIII, 95.

ence to the President, Claude, Florence chooses a young man
of no importance, who appeals to her because, as she says, "he
is the god of small misfortunes" (p. 92). This phrase puzzled
the critics, who saw in him only a happy-go-lucky idler.[30] A
close reading of the text leaves a different impression. As Florence explains to Claude: "He [Jérôme] is dexterous, ingenious,
industrious. He will solve existence as one solves a Chinese
puzzle, with his hands. His future lies in mechanics and electricity. . . . He is a pure creature, free of worries, free of memories. And he is free of age" (pp. 103–104). This passage seems
to imply that Jérôme is a member of the working class, in contrast to Claude who represents the powers that be. If one recalls
that the working class enjoyed a brief moment of power under
Léon Blum during the Popular Front Government directly preceding that of Daladier, Florence's break with Claude in favor
of Jérôme is a typical Giralducian allegory. Like *Siegfried*, its
political significance was lost on all save the initiates, largely
because the author was so far removed from the reality of workers and revolutionaries that he was unable to depict them con-
vincingly. There is an amusing allusion to the proletariat in the
original version of *Siegfried* which shows to what extent Giraudoux envisaged it in metaphorical terms: "It's curious: the prole-
tarians all have in their pockets the means to plug themselves
into electric power. A proletarian is a liaison agent of electricity.
The great day will be the day they find the right dynamo; it
will be Electric Day!"[31] Even that metaphor is rather hermetic
unless it is related to the story of André Marty, the electrical
engineer who led the Black Sea Rebellion during the war of
intervention against Russia in 1919. The campaign to free the
insubordinate sailors was in full force during the writing of

[30] Henri Bidou, in *Marianne*, October 26, 1938.
[31] *Théâtre Complet*, I, 142.

Siegfried et le Limousin, in which there are veiled allusions to those events.[32]

If Giraudoux's rare evocations of the working class lack verisimilitude, the reasons are that he despised the technique of realist writing and that he had no illusions about the ability of the bourgeois writer to depict working-class reality. He states this very succinctly in his essay on Charles-Louis Philippe:

> If what we call realism is, for the writer, the fact of expressing reality, we may then say that the French writer has more chance to achieve it the further he moves away from the common people, the feelings of those people, or nature, in the strictest sense. By the very fact of his training and the exclusive nature of his brotherhood, he is as qualified to encounter that reality of the people, which he takes as his subject, as the seminarist leaving Saint Sulpice is to encounter the god Pan. Every time an age is dual and confused, when anarchy and revolution steal into the arteries of the nation, our literature is then real only to the extent that it expresses not those movements themselves but the reactions of the bourgeois order and the individual bourgeois in relation to them. But whether it be Balzac's peasants or Vallès' workers, their authenticity is achieved only when the authors do not try to cross the boundary of the peasant and working-class world and soul. The novels of our realists and our populists, when they portray a mason or a farmer, are no more than crude decalcomanias—tuppence colored-sheets for bourgeois, next to which a novel by Octave Feuillet constitutes, as far as the bourgeois soul is concerned, a magnificent collection of truths. At the very most, they achieve reality at a point midway between: at the middleman, the steward, the foreman.[33]

---

[32] ". . . for it was thanks to similar knots that, during the revolution, they recognized and arrested the sailors, who were then all communists" (p. 62); ". . . what he hated the most were electrical engineers and sidewalk artists . . ." (p. 238).

[33] *Littérature,* p. 111.

Even if one is of the opinion that Giraudoux judged the realism of Balzac or Vallès too harshly, one can only be grateful
that he did not parade his Jérôme across the set of *La Folle de
Chaillot* except in the person of the happy-go-lucky character
who brightens the stage for a moment with his song. The picturesque characters who are natural to the setting—the waitress,
the ragpicker, the street singer, the flower girl—are much closer
to the working-class reality than the shadowy Jérôme and perfectly in tune with the rest of the play.

Giraudoux's antirealist treatment of the characters in *La Folle
de Chaillot* is even more evident in his caricature of the profiteers. The curtain goes up on the President and the Baron seated
at a table of the Café Francis and engaged in earnest conversation. This is not the dignified and courtly president of *Cantique
des Cantiques;* the President of *La Folle de Chaillot* is the head
of numerous corporations, and he is offering the Baron a seat on
the board of directors of a new company which he has just
founded. They introduce themselves to each other and to the
audience with a brief history of their criminal records. The
Baron is a self-confessed failure who has had to sell his estate
to pay for his dissolute living and who is now reduced to lend-
ing his name and his services to shady financial dealings. The
President discloses how he climbed the ladder all the way from
petty thefts to gigantic swindles. He made the jump from rags
to riches by allying himself with a certain type of individual
whom he could single out by his face:

> I turned to those impressive and nameless faces I had noticed
> stationed in the midst of the crowd, watching indifferently. My
> fortune was made. A first smooth, hairless face, encountered right
> in the subway, gave me the opportunity of earning my first real
> thousand francs by passing off counterfeit hundred-sou pieces.
> Another one, which I found on the Place de l'Opéra, just as
> smooth and hairless but with strawberry marks, gave scope to

my talent by entrusting me with the management of a gang selling fake flashlight batteries. I had caught on. And since then, I had merely to give myself over to those lifeless masks . . . to become what you now see me: president of eleven companies, a member of fifty-two boards of directors, the holder of as many bank accounts, and chairman of the board of the cartel in which you have just accepted a directorship.

The portrait of the President and his associates is drawn with the exaggerated and simplistic lines of caricature, which creates a face to evoke a personality. Giraudoux adopts this technique to dramatic action in an unexpected way. While the President is trying to find a name for the corporations which he has just founded, he breaks off suddenly, exclaiming: "Look! Over there! That's one. And I've never seen a more promising one!"

THE BARON: A woman? Where do you see women?

THE PRESIDENT: A face. One of those faces I was telling you about. That man sitting to our left, who's drinking water.

THE BARON: Promising! It looks like a post!

THE PRESIDENT: Just as you say. One of those signposts of human trickery, greed, human obstinacy. They are planted all along the roads of gambling, steel, lechery, phosphate. They are landmarks on the way to success, prison, and power. Look. He's already noticed us. And understood. He's going to come over.

The Baron, watching uneasily, is surprised to see the President ready to betray their secrets to a stranger, but the President reassures him, saying: "Those twisted lips, those shifty eyes, are, in our professional circles, the guarantees of loyalty, our brand of loyalty. Besides, he has recognized me, too. And he won't hesitate, either, to disclose everything to me" (p. 14).

The President is not the only character who is able to distinguish in the crowd one of those faces that should not belong to the human race. The ragpicker, too, knows how to recognize them and picks up the theme of the face: "In the past, when you walked around Paris, the people you met were like you. . . . But ten years ago, one day, in the street, I suddenly felt sick. Among the passers-by I saw a man who had nothing in common with the usual ones. He was stocky, potbellied; his right eye was leering, his left eye shifty; another race . . ." (p. 61). Then he explains to the madwomen that since then there has been a veritable invasion of these new creatures, who do not live like the rest of mankind:

> They have no trade. When they meet, they whisper and slip each other five-thousand-franc notes. You find them near the Stock Exchange, but they don't shout; near blocks of houses that are going to be torn down, but they don't work; near the piles of cabbages in the Central Market, but they don't touch them; in front of cinemas, but they watch the people in line, they don't go in. In the past, consumer goods, plays, seemed to sell themselves, to display themselves. Now, all foodstuffs, all entertainment, all business ventures, both wines and shows—you'd think they had some pimp who puts them out on the sidewalk and watches over them, without doing a thing. (pp. 62–63)

This tirade against the financier, who traffics in everything from wines to plays, may have been inspired in part by the fate of *Judith*.[34] In all probability, Giraudoux's hatred of this tribe and his desire for revenge stem from this episode, but his discovery of this new race goes back to an earlier period.

At the end of 1926 Giraudoux published a booklet entitled *Les Hommes-tigres,* which does not seem to have created much of a stir. At any rate, I found no mention of it in the press. Either the critics were unaware of its existence or they deliberately ignored it. *Les Hommes-tigres* begins as a tale related in the first person. The setting is the Café de Cluny where the author has a rendezvous with Dagot, an administrator from the Congo. Every three and one-half years Dagot has six months

34 See p. 129.

leave, which he spends in Paris. He and the narrator are old acquaintances, and they look forward to these regular reunions. This one is suddenly broken off in the middle of a sentence when Dagot's attention is distracted by a face he sees at the neighboring table:

> He was staring at someone at a nearby table, sitting sideways on his chair and almost facing us. . . . I now had before me, not the friend who was taking some relaxation, the colonial at rest whom I had known, but the master of forests, wild beasts, cannibals. . . .
> "Look at our neighbor's eyes," he told me.
> In the past, the coachmen in Paris had epithets to designate those passers-by grazed by their cabs who gave the impression of being abstractions. . . . Cholera. . . . The plague. . . . But never had abstraction inhabited a man as much as it did our neighbor; his eyes did not seem to belong to his face. On that pale visage, beneath thin, blonde hair . . . the eye was drawn on whited wood, the eye of an idol. . . .[35]

Dagot is so struck by the resemblance between this face and the members of a secret society of cannibals disguised as "tiger-men," whom he has been tracking down in the Congo, that he excuses himself and leaves precipitately in pursuit of the stranger. The implication is that Paris, too, has its cannibals or tiger-men. The history of this odd little tale and the variant forms in which it can be found, not only in Giraudoux's works but also under different titles and authors, will be the subject of a separate chapter, but *Les Hommes-tigres* is of interest here because of the resemblance between the officers of the corporation and the initiates of the secret society of cannibals, both of whom can be identified by their facial characteristics.

In the first version of *La Folle de Chaillot* it did not occur to Giraudoux to use the intriguing device of *Les Hommes-tigres*. The rough draft of the first scene introduces three characters in-

[35] *Les Hommes-tigres* (Emile-Paul, 1926), pp. 16–17.

stead of two: the President, the Prospector, and the Academician. This trio represents what Jean de Pierrefeu called "the capitalist cell"[36]—the moneyed people, the adventurers in grand larceny, the alliance between members of that bulwark of tradition, the Académie Française and the remnants of the aristocracy. The role of the Academician is to disinfect Chaillot of the specters that haunt it, thus making the district more favorable for prospection. The Prospector suggests that the Academician write a book about them or bring the artists into Chaillot! This is an allusion to Louis Dumur, whose novel, *Les Défaitistes* (1923), brought fame to the Café de la Rotonde and exorcised the specters of Trotsky and Mata Hari with cubist painters and *avant-garde* writers. Subsequently, Giraudoux replaced the role of the Academician with that of the Baron, who shows unmistakably the collusion between the aristocracy and the corporation. But it is in the role of the Prospector that Giraudoux made the most significant change, one that allowed him to adapt for the stage the device that appears in *Les Hommes-tigres*. Instead of showing all three members of the notorious trio on stage when the curtain goes up, he delayed the appearance of the Prospector by having the President single him out among the customers at the bar in somewhat the same way as Dagot spotted his tiger-man in the Café de Cluny—by that lifeless mask which marks the members of secret societies, whether in Paris or Gabon. This seemingly minor revision had the dual advantage of tightening the dramatic action and accentuating the lines of the caricature.

By creating the role of the Broker, Giraudoux added yet another caricature to the grotesque trio of the Baron, the President, and the Prospector. The Broker's rapid-fire account of the stock market operations that are contemplated for the new corporation bear a certain resemblance to the terrorist methods de-

[36] See the table of contents of *L'Anti-Plutarque* (Paris: Editions de France, 1925).

scribed in Dagot's report on the practices of the tiger-men. Giraudoux puts the finishing touches on his caricature when he has
the Prospector demand, as a pledge of loyalty, that each one
recount one swindle that he perpetrated at the cost of human
life. The President boasts of having sunk a ship insured for three
times its value. The Baron claims that he blackmailed a young
girl until she committed suicide. The Broker claims to have
pocketed a good share of the funds he had collected for the
benefit of flood victims in southern France. Such is the diabolical
brotherhood that is plotting to blow up Paris in order to prospect
for oil.

No subtlety or shading is evident in Giraudoux's statement of
the problem. Everything is black and white, like his caricature
of the profiteers. So also is the response of the Madwoman. Formerly, Aurélie believed that the power of illusion would suffice
to make the world happy and beautiful. This is the philosophy
which Giraudoux illustrated in such an amusing fashion in
L'Apollon de Bellac, admitting in the end that it was a form
of cowardice. But when Aurélie is finally convinced by the Ragpicker that the profiteers are plotting to destroy Chaillot and
eventually all of Paris, she is ready for action. With the terrible
logic of madness, she reasons that profiteers are by definition
greedy and that they are, therefore, naive. By baiting them with
the smell of oil, she plans to bury them alive in the subsoil of
Chaillot that they are planning to prospect. First, she summons
the sewerman to her basement apartment on Chaillot Street to
have him show her how to open and close the door to a subterranean passage leading from her living quarters. This done,
she takes counsel with her friends, Constance, Gabrielle, and
Josephine, three madwomen from different quarters of Paris. The
quartet of madwomen parallels the four profiteers of the first act
and is doubtless a substitute for the four seventeenth-century
writers who appear in one of the variants. As a matter of fact,

the four madwomen are a rather transparent disguise for some twentieth-century writers who may have convened in this very location during the Occupation. The Madwoman of Chaillot is very likely a composite of Louis Aragon and Jean Giraudoux.[37] The names of André Beucler and Pierre Lestringuez actually appear in another variant of the play,[38] where it is indicated that they were clients of the Café Francis. Certain details in the play, such as Constance's peculiar habit of barricading herself in her room and obliging her friends to mew three times like a cat before she will open her door (p. 90), can be found in the writings of Jean de Pierrefeu, whom Giraudoux may also have had in mind when he created the madwomen.[39]

Between the lines of banter, Aurélie states the problem, presents her solution and enlists the support of her friends. There is no indecision or soul-searching in their deliberations such as that which characterizes the anarchists in the dramas of Sartre and Camus.[40] Aurélie's one concern is to give some appearance of legality to the proceedings. Her confessor has already given her his blessing. When she confessed her desire to kill all the wicked people in the world, he replied blandly: "Don't deny yourself that, my child. When you have made up your mind, I shall lend

[37] See p. 134.

[38] *Théâtre complet*, XVI, *Variantes*, IV, 150.

[39] *Dix ans après, Horoscopes futuristes de quelques notables contemporains* (Ferenczi, 1930), p. 173. This detail can be found in the chapter entitled "Moeurs judiciares, un grand avocat en 1940." The chapter is most probably a caricature of Poincaré. It is concerned with certain habits that are related to the use Poincaré made of publicity to win his trials. The detail of the old woman is part of the memoirs of a client—a murderer—which the lawyer had published in *Le Matin:* "Very good, that passage in your *Memoirs,* the murder of the old woman of means from Vésinet, the idea of imitating the mewing of a cat to attract the old woman outside; all that is astonishingly picturesque." Jean de Pierrefeu was a friend of long standing who started out in the world of journalism at the same time as Giraudoux.

[40] Camus' *Les Justes* and Sartre's *Les Mains sales.*

you the jawbone of Samson's ass" (p. 94). The legal side of the question is handled by Josephine, who, like Lestringuez, has studied law. She declares that murder is justified by law only when one kills en masse. All wars are based on this principle; hence, the draft and compulsory military service (p. 100). Witness the Flood and the destruction of Sodom and Gomorrah by the Archangels. There is only one necessary condition to Aurélie's plan to exterminate the profiteers; they must be defended by a lawyer before they can be condemned to death (p. 101). Since time is short, Aurélie decides to call on the first passerby, who happens to be the Ragpicker. He is invited to plead the case of the profiteers so that the four madwomen can hand down a verdict without scaring off their victims, who are due to arrive shortly. The Ragpicker's impromptu defense of money before what he sardonically calls "the elite and elegant public" (p. 108) is a masterpiece of irony. Aurélie quickly sums up the case by stating that money is the root of all evil and calls for the verdict. The Ragpicker, still playing his role, protests that as a member of the two hundred families he is not subject to any laws, but Aurélie demands full powers from her allies to eliminate all the exploiters from the world. Her demand is granted by shouts of approbation (p. 117). At this point a procession of presidents, prospectors, and advertisers files past equipped with a goldbrick and papers to sign giving them the right to lock Aurélie up in an insane asylum and pocket all the profits. Irma, the waitress, offers them a glass of water flavored with gasoline, which intoxicates them with anticipation of the riches they expect to find in Aurélie's basement. As they rush headlong into the subterranean passage, like the thieves of Ali Baba, three women arrive who have heard rumors of the deal and want to get in on it. Aurélie obligingly lets them through before sealing off the passage forever.

A happy throng of little people descends to thank Aurélie for their deliverance and to tell how wonderful it is to live in a world free of exploiters. Then from the opposite wall of her apartment comes a procession of specters that have been liberated by her action, the friends of the happy plants and animals. This last scene recalls a passage from *Siegfried et le Limousin:*

> I do not wish to die before having seen Europe happy once again. Without having seen the reappearance of that review, whose director's whereabouts are unknown to me, *The International Echo of Happy People,* with its illustrated supplement of happy animals and plants, and its three hundred subscribers. Without having seen the two words which an invincible force separates more each day, the word Russia and the word Happiness, meet on my lips once again. (p. 174)

Giraudoux did not live to see his wish fulfilled, but in writing *La Folle de Chaillot* he contributed in his own inimitable way to realizing his dream of a happy Europe. He describes his objective in the variant of the first act where he evokes the phantoms of the classical writers, Nicolas Boileau, Jean Racine, and Jean de la Fontaine.

> NICOLAS: You're dreaming, Jean!
> JEAN: Maybe. But what does it matter, if we get the world to dream with us! That's all it asks for. You heard that lady, who was holding the young man by the arm. She changes her irises into roses, her house into a castle, her life into adventure. One has only to put trust in men and nature, Nicolas, for them to turn our dreams into realities.

This faith in the will to illusion was somewhat shaken by the events of 1940. Until then Giraudoux had believed, rightly or wrongly, that the "enumeration of the pure is not a plebiscite but a secret."[41] He preferred to follow the advice of Schiller to remain pure in the midst of all impurities and steadfast despite

---

[41] *Pour ce onze novembre* (Paris: Grasset, 1938), p. 8.

all the changes in the outer world.[42] After the defeat he admitted in *Sans Pouvoirs* that "individual integrity never redeemed, for a people or a corporation, the general corruption" (p. 87). Giraudoux realized that his cardinal sin was timidity and that in refusing to speak out he was, in part, responsible for the disaster.

In *La Folle de Chaillot* he created a character that symbolizes his timidity and his shrinking from bold action. The Madwoman had a lover, Adolphe Bertaut, who never had the courage to marry her. In one of the dream sequences at the end of the play, a procession of Adolphe Bertauts appears carrying the melon he snatched from under her nose when they met by chance at a fruit market. The phantoms make the following pathetic little speech: "We are all the Adolph Bertauts of the world. We have decided to conquer that timidity which has ruined our life and yours. We shall no longer flee what we love. We shall no longer follow what we hate" (p. 138). This symbolic offering of the melon with a proposal of marriage expresses Giraudoux's desire to make a fresh start and find the courage to act in accordance with his convictions. He died before his resolution could be put to the test, and it was his friends and associates who had to produce *La Folle de Chaillot* with its unequivocal indictment of the profiteers.

The critics were variously annoyed, embarrassed, and even a little indignant, though no one dared to attack the dead poet openly. Some saw it as a pamphlet, written in the blackest ink. However, the public of the extreme left was irritated by the cloak of madness and fantasy which he assumed and disappointed that he was not more militant in expressing his ideas. Such light and humorous treatment of so serious a theme seemed inappropriate to the militant revolutionary, as the rightist press

[42] Johann Schiller, *Poésie naive et sentimentale,* trans. and introd. Robert Leroux (Aubier, 1947).

noted with some satisfaction.[43] But the critic who expressed most accurately, it would seem, the reaction of the general public is the one who saw the play as a "charming and profound entertainment, in which the aspirations of a people are so well expressed":

> This biting and violent demand for freedom and the pursuit of happiness, this healthy reaction to the victory of venality and the will to power, Giraudoux has skillfully disguised as an entertainment. An entertainment which is not exactly a comedy. . . . Giraudoux, we have understood your final message. May God give our country many such madmen as Aurélie, the Madwoman of Chaillot.[44]

For those who had been the closest to Giraudoux, *La Folle de Chaillot* was something of a revelation, which frightened and astonished them by its unequivocal message. In a newspaper interview published a week before the opening night, Pierre Lestringuez warned the public: "Thank God, I don't have to tell you about this truculent and bitter fantasy, intoxicated with justice, which I know so well. I envy your having the pleasure of discovering it and hearing the arguments of that imperious poetry of the great moralists, of those who have had the privilege of departing this world while leaving to mankind, for eternity, the piercing echo of their laughter."[45]

Giraudoux's laughter is that of a man who has finally squared his accounts with those powers who are responsible for war, poverty, ugliness—in short, for the world's misery. His laughter is also directed against the venal press, which is the enemy of free speech and artistic expression. He well knew that he had chosen the one time in this half-century when he could speak out and purge himself of his desire for revolt. His laughter rises

---

[43] Thierry Maulnier, in *Essor*, January 5, 1946.
[44] S. Genest, in *Témoignage chrétien*, December 28, 1945.
[45] *XXᵉ Siècle*, December 13, 1945.

above his personal motives for revenge and stems primarily from
the feelings of a patriot, sardonically exposing those who pros-
tituted and betrayed his country. It is the laughter of a pure
heart and a lucid mind that understood the direction of history
and his century:

> Let me laugh when I hear it proclaimed that France is to be, here
> below, the organ of restraint and level-headedness! The destiny of
> France is to be a thorn in the flesh of the world. She has been
> created, she has created herself, to frustrate the conspiracy of es-
> tablished roles, of eternal systems in the world. She is justice, but
> only to the extent that justice consists in condemning those who
> have been right for too long. She is good sense, but only when
> good sense is the denouncer, the righter of wrongs, the avenger.
> As long as there is a France worthy of that name, the game of the
> universe will never be played out, the newly successful nations will
> not rest easy, whether they have won their rank by work, force,
> or trade. In order, in tranquility, in wealth, there is an element
> insulting to mankind and to freedom, which France is there to
> point out and to punish.[46]

This outburst dates from 1937 when, under the Popular Front
Government, Giraudoux felt more confident of his country's
destiny and freer to express his democratic sentiments. This side
of Giraudoux's character was generally underestimated and
somewhat of a mystery even to those who worked most closely
with him. Louis Jouvet himself bears witness to this in the program notes he wrote for *La Folle de Chaillot*,[47] addressing them
to the deceased writer. "A new light illumines your writings,"
Jouvet says. In this remarkable statement by Giraudoux's chief

---

[46] *L'Impromptu de Paris, Théâtre complet*, VIII, 65–66. Giraudoux put
these words into the mouth of Louis Jouvet, who is in the process of
explaining the role of the theatre and of France to the deputy Robineau.
The latter had drafted a bill requesting a large appropriation for the
dramatic arts.

[47] See Appendix IV.

mentor, director, and producer, there is a strange admission. He begins by apologizing for not having kept the rendezvous of October 17, which Giraudoux had jokingly inscribed on the manuscript. Jouvet explains that this delay of several weeks in the production of the play is unimportant and is due to any number of good reasons. There is another delay, however, that is not so readily excusable. We have been slow to understand the real meaning of our gestures and occupations, states Jouvet, adding that Giraudoux's death creates in each of his works a message that needs to be clarified. Each of his plays seems to anticipate and announce something; each one gives evidence of Giraudoux's prophetic insight. Since the revelation of *La Folle de Chaillot,* new perspectives are opening up, and new conjectures are forced upon us.

Jouvet's singular admission, which I have paraphrased here, that he was only beginning to grasp the full import of Giraudoux's theatre, made little impression on the critics. One is somewhat shocked to read Sartre's terse dismissal of Giraudoux as a thinker in those stimulating critical essays, *Qu'est-ce que la littérature?,* which date from 1947. "I know that Giraudoux always said, 'The only question is to find one's style. The idea comes afterward.' But he was wrong. The idea never came."[48] To whom did the idea never come? It is forgivable to have written in 1944 that Giraudoux died "carrying away with him the key to that useless world into which men no longer wish to enter."[49] *Sodome et Gomorrhe* is, indeed, a discouraging poetic testament, but the existence of *La Folle de Chaillot* sheds a new light on all of Giraudoux's writings, as Louis Jouvet was the first to point out.

If Giraudoux's ideas and objectives were not evident even to the keenest critical minds of two generations, Gide and Sartre,

[48] *Situations II,* p. 76.
[49] "Hommage à Giraudoux," *Comoedia,* February 5, 1944.

it is perhaps because militant literature is identified in the minds of most Frenchmen with the style of Voltaire. Giraudoux's aesthetics would seem to be at cross-purposes with the aim of the committed writer—in fact, with his own aim. At one point Giraudoux stated that the role of the dramatist is analogous to that of the actor. He must be the speech organ of his age.[50] Elsewhere he claimed that the modern writer must be like a journalist, in touch with current events.[51] This does not mean, however, that he must write like a journalist. The creative artist can be the voice of his age without being representational. In fact, the competition of photography and the news media forces him to create art forms which are the antithesis of realism. The creative artist must communicate, but not exclusively through the conscious mind of his public. "The theatre is not a theorem, but a spectacle; not a lesson, but a filter,"[52] Giraudoux maintained. He never lost sight of the fact that theatregoers demanded entertainment, not sermons or diatribes. So the more urgent the message he wanted to convey, the droller became his comedy, the more eloquent and sparkling his dialogue, and the more elaborate the spectacle which he prepared for his public.

[50] *Littérature*, p. 243.
[51] See p. 119.
[52] *Théâtre complet*, VIII, 44.

✦ VII ✦

Les Hommes-tigres

Shortly after the First World War, a small group of men became aware of a serious danger threatening the world, specifically, the colonial world; namely, the threat of anthropophagy. As concerned citizens, they called the matter to the attention of the authorities, who ignored it. Determined to be heard, they found a more sympathetic ear in the Fathers of the Holy Ghost, a Catholic mission in the Congo, which published the warning in its organ, the *Annales apostoliques des P. P. du Saint Esprit* in the March–April 1921 issue (pp. 50–58). The article, entitled "L'Homme-tigre," was signed: H.C., colonial administrator. It was presented under the heading "French Congo" with an introductory note, presumably written by the administrator H.C., explaining why the latter was addressing the article to the reverend fathers instead of to the civil authorities: "The Colonial Administration is not concerned with the Tiger-Man: the Tiger-Man is part of the native customs, which must be left untouched. In fact, this matter, they believe, does not affect either taxes or manpower, which are the only two things worthy of their interest. This report was addressed, in its time, to the Colonial Administration; the latter, naturally, took no notice of it." The report is dated November 26, 1916.

The article contains a detailed account of the practices of a secret society of so-called tiger-men, who are, to use a less figurative language, cannibals. The precision of the report is at once admirable and terrifying: the society's organization, meetings, deliberations, bylaws, initiation rites, warning system, and objectives are set forth with the utmost clarity and in the dry and incisive style of a man accustomed to drawing up official reports. The author concludes by saying: "I shall not dwell on the consequences, for the future of the country, to which such practices would lead, nor on the necessity for strenuously checking them. The creation, here and now, of a temporary post in the midst of the regions on which this society is exerting its influence is urgently required; it is a matter of no less than half the subdivision."

We do not know whether or not the recommendation of H.C. was acted upon, but the appearance of another article in the *Annales* three years later entitled "A precise testimony concerning the recent facts of anthropophagy" (July–August 1924) indicates that H.C. was no longer a voice crying out in the wilderness. This article by an unknown author treats a case of cannibalism in the village of Victoria, where English tradesmen had opened factories, and some of the details of the testimony recall those of H.C.'s report on the "tiger-men" of Gabon.

Not content with the modest stir they created in the *Annals of the Fathers of the Holy Ghost,* the instigators of the crusade against cannibalism renewed their efforts to obtain the support of the Colonial Administration. By a happy coincidence, in 1922, a society was organized for the purpose of founding an official bulletin entitled *Les Recherches Congolaises.* The Governor General of Equatorial Africa, Victor Augagneur, was the founder of the society and the bulletin was published in Brazzaville by the government printing office. The purpose of the society, as stated by its perpetual secretary, Julien Maigret, in the preface to the first issue, was to rescue from oblivion native African customs and vestiges of an ephemeral past. Its membership was not restricted to scholars; it was open to anyone "who, having lived in the Congo, had observed its people and things, and to all those who, for any reason whatever, were interested in the colony." Such a broadminded editorial policy was likely to attract a wide variety of contributions, and it did; but the subject which seemed to be of primary interest to the editors of the *Recherches Congolaises* was an investigation of the African secret societies.

The first article, "Notes sur les Kakas de la circonscription de l'Ibenga-Likoula," by a colonial administrator named Darré, contains a startling reference to "panther-men," whom he calls witch doctors. However, he does not hesitate to repeat some of the legends about them: "According to some, their name comes from the fact that the totem of this tribe is the panther—according to others, any candidate for the secret sect has to clothe himself in a panther skin, paint his body in striped patterns, and put small knives on each of his fingers in order to kidnap the victim for the initiates' soup."[1]

Unfortunately, Darré is unable to give any more exact information about this fascinating subject, but he expresses the hope that further research will reveal precise details of the rites and practices of the panther-men. The issue concludes with a request for information on a number of topics, among which are the secret societies of Ubangi. Apparently, there was no response to this particular request; so in order to encourage an investigation of these secret societies, the editors published in the second issue of the *Recherches Congolaises* a questionnaire on African ethnology prepared by Georges Foucart.

Darré contributed another article in the third issue of the *Recherches Congolaises,* this time on the customs of the Bondjo tribe. In it he refers again to the fetish of the panther as a form of witchcraft, adding that it was impossible to obtain any infor-

[1] *Recherches Congolaises,* No. 1 (1922), pp. 17–19.

mation on the subject.[2] At the end of this issue the editors repeat their request: "We once again urgently appeal to our cor-
respondents to furnish us with the information requested in the
two previous issues of the bulletin, on the secret societies of
Ubangi. Please refer back to the detailed questionnaire inserted
under this heading in issue No. 2." But the year 1923 passed
without bringing the editors of the *Recherches Congolaises* the
much needed information. In the fifth issue Reverend Father J.
Rémy, a missionary of the Holy Ghost, published an article entitled "Fétiches et féticheurs," which recalls the importance of
the problem:

> Finally, let us mention, in conclusion, the secret societies, which
> have such a great influence on the population of Africa. Their ob-
> jective appears to be that of preserving the customs of the tribe, by
> imposing their will on the women, slaves, children, and the un-
> initiated and forcing them to work. They are used by the political
> and religious leaders for carrying out secret decisions and for get-
> ting rid of nuisances. Today some are used to procure wealth by
> various means. And there, also, is where the plots against the
> white man are hatched.[3]

If we can believe the Reverend Father's testimony, it would
have been to the interest of the colonial administrators to con-
duct an investigation of such societies. This was surely the
opinion of the bulletin's editors, for at the end of this issue
there is still another appeal:

> We again call to the attention of our correspondents the detailed
> questionnaire inserted under this same heading in issue No. 2 of
> our bulletin. It would be of great interest to have information
> about the secret societies of Ubangi or of other parts of French
> Equatorial Africa. We are counting on the good will of our con-

[2] *Ibid.*, No. 3 (1923), p. 70.
[3] *Ibid.*, No. 5 (1924), pp. 100–101.

tributors to undertake this important study and to pass on to us the results of their research.

The study that the editors had been requesting since the founding of the *Recherches Congolaises* was finally published in the sixth issue. Under the heading "Varieties" the following item appears: "Our inquiry into the secret societies, excerpt of a letter from M. Charbonnier, assistant to the Civil Service, dated Tchibanga, November 26, 1916."[4] Charbonnier's letter treats "the Secret Society of panther-men in the Bouyala territory." In spite of the new title and a few minor changes, this is essentially the same text, almost in its entirety, that was published in the *Annales apostoliques des P. P. du Saint Esprit* four years previously by the administrator H.C., who is undoubtedly the Monsieur Charbonnier of the *Recherches Congolaises*. Why the editors were so anxious to publish a study that was made nearly ten years ago and which had already been published in another journal that was well known to its contributors is a matter for conjecture. The fact that the editors of the *Recherches Congolaises* dropped the question altogether after publishing Charbonnier's letter makes their urgent appeals for information on secret societies a little suspect. On the other hand, it is possible that H.C.'s report covered the subject so thoroughly that no further research was needed. A comparison of this document with the little that had already been published on the secret societies of Africa reveals an intimate and detailed knowledge such as no trained anthropologist had been able to produce.

In spite of the timeliness of the subject and the precise and lurid details contained in Charbonnier's letter, despite the support of an official organ of the Colonial Administration and a Catholic missionary order, the crusade against cannibalism might have bogged down entirely had it not come to the at-

[4] *Ibid.* (1925, first quarter), pp. 171–181.

tention of the Paris office of the Information and Press Service,[5] which was headed at that time by Jean Giraudoux. He seems to have understood the implications of Charbonnier's report and judged that it deserved a wider circulation. Rather than risk having it gather dust in the Colonial Office across the way, Giraudoux decided to publish it under his own name and embellished it with a fictionalized introduction that was certain to intrigue the reader. The booklet appeared toward the end of 1926 under the title, *Les Hommes-tigres,* which is almost identical with that of H.C.'s article in the *Annales.* The author of the report figures in the story under the name of Dagot and is presented as an old acquaintance of the narrator, who is presumably Jean Giraudoux. The rendezvous between these two men at the Café de Cluny has already been related in the preceding chapter.[6] We may recall that Dagot's attention had been distracted by the face of a man sitting at the next table. Dagot had suddenly stopped speaking to stare at someone. Giraudoux, who turned to look, saw a face pale as whited wood with the eye of an idol. Suddenly the object of their attention got up and left, whereupon Dagot excused himself hastily, saying, "They are the same eyes. . ." and dashed off in pursuit of the stranger. The next day Giraudoux received a letter containing a copy of an official report drawn up by Dagot with an enigmatic note of explanation: "Dear friend, I'm on the trail of something. Do forgive my hasty departure. I caught the man, and what a business! As for the letter, it is very short. Eyes like that can't be misleading. I shall tell you all about it four years from now."[7] The reader had to wait nearly twenty years before Giraudoux

[5] The office of the Information and Press Service was in the same building as the Colonial Office, 20 rue de la Boétie.

[6] See pp. 140–143.

[7] *Les Hommes-tigres,* présentés par Jean Giraudoux. (Paris: Emile-Paul, 1926), p. 46.

was to provide a clue to the mystery. It was not until the curtain went up on that same smooth hairless face in the first act of *La Folle de Chaillot* that it was possible for the uninitiated to have an inkling of what Dagot was talking about.

We are only beginning to unravel the mystification of *Les Hommes-tigres,* however. The key to the work is the theme of the face, which is introduced by the President when he picks up the Prospector and echoed by the Ragpicker in his famous speech, "Le monde file un mauvais coton." (The world is in a bad way). Dagot had made his big discovery in the same way as the President and the Ragpicker. Not only does the theme of the face figure in Giraudoux's fictionalized introduction, but it is incorporated in Charbonnier's report on the secret society of tiger-men:

> Finally, the members of this Society have neither a password, nor signs, nor identifying marks. They recognize each other, it appears, by an expression in the eyes. Indeed, I have noticed, in the features of these people, something special: at a time when I still knew nothing precise about this society, I apprehended at one fell blow, by using the census and by looking the people in the face, six tiger-men out of the ten men presented, and I was not wrong about one of them. As a matter of fact, it is to the accuracy of this move that I owe all the disclosures I have collected in this report.[8]

Both Giraudoux and the colonial administrator Charbonnier had a remarkable faculty for identifying members of secret societies by their facial characteristics, be they cannibals or crooks. This device Giraudoux used effectively in fiction and on stage, but its appearance in an official report is curious. Charbonnier's letter as printed in the *Recherches Congolaises* and even Giraudoux's booklet, *Les Hommes-tigres,* have been taken seriously

---

[8] Henceforth all quotations from the Charbonnier report will be taken from Giraudoux's version in *Les Hommes-tigres.* For this one, see pp. 28–29.

by the bibliographers as an important source of anthropological facts. The *Bibliographie ethnographique du Congo Belge et des régions avoisinantes*[9] contains the following critical notice of Charbonnier's letter: "Important communication on the secret societies of the Bayaka in the Tchibanga region of French Equatorial Africa. The information has reference to the leopard-men who form a secret society, of which Maghéna is the fetish and which has rites and laws" (p. 65). It is even more astonishing to find Giraudoux's booklet, *Les Hommes-tigres,* catalogued at the Bibliothèque Nationale with the works on anthropology.

These two important ethnological and anthropological communications contain some baffling discrepancies. Charbonnier estimates the proportion of panther-men in Ubangi to be as high as sixty per cent of the native population, which is an alarming figure. However, Dagot's account gives a similar statistic for the neighboring territory of Gabon, which would indicate that these practices were fairly widespread in French Equatorial Africa. But the conclusion of *Les Hommes-tigres* gives the impression that Paris too has its share of cannibals. In other words, the secret society of tiger-men is not limited in its operations to any particular locale. The crusade would seem to be directed at a general phenomenon that is not restricted to the French colonies.

The shifting locale of the two versions is more readily explained than the shifting terminology. Panthers, leopards, and even lions are terms that can be used interchangeably, but the tiger is generally associated with the Asian continent and would hardly be appropriate in this context. Yet the first version published in the *Annales* dealt with *l'homme-tigre.* In the version Charbonnier submitted to the *Recherches Congolaises,* he prudently changed the term to *l'homme-panthère.* Then when Giraudoux lent his name to the crusade, he reverted to the term of the original article and entitled his booklet *Les Hommes-*

[9] Brussels (Falk Fils, 1925–30), p. 65.

tigres. To the European, obviously, the man-eating tiger is a more familiar symbol of cannibalism than the leopard or the panther, but Charbonnier is allegedly dealing with facts, not symbols.

In any event, no one would seem to have attacked the authenticity of either Charbonnier's article or Giraudoux's booklet. On the contrary, in 1928 the *Recherches Congolaises* published a two-page article by M. de Muraz on "Les Superstitions dans la race Sara," in which he describes a society of "lion-men." Again in 1929 there appeared an account of proceedings against several "panther-men," but the interrogation established nothing so conclusive as Charbonnier's report. No direct reference to the latter appeared until 1931 when a Lieutenant Regondeau submitted a "Contribution à l'étude de l'homme-tigre," in which he also alludes to Giraudoux's book on the subject. This article traces the origins of the secret society to the superstition of the werewolf, which is part of the legendary lore of certain regions of France, in particular the Beauce and Auvergne. Although Regondeau assures the reader that he has no wish to cast doubts on Giraudoux's good faith, he implies that the phenomenon of the "tiger-man" may be more imaginary than real. However, he says, this proves only that the reality of the African native is different from ours: the former is often incapable of distinguishing between fact and the phantoms of his imagination.

Neither Charbonnier nor Giraudoux deigned to reply to the polite aspersions cast upon their findings. Instead, the Charbonnier report was submitted to another official journal, the *Bulletin de l'Agence économique de l'Afrique équatoriale,* published in Paris. Unlike the *Recherches Congolaises,* this journal is an important source of information relating to trade and industry. Its format is impressive and its articles are buttressed with statistical tables. However, it did occasionally use as filler the sort of material solicited by the *Recherches Congolaises.* The fables of

Father Walker, for example, and articles by E. Eboué on the beliefs and rites of the peoples of Ubangi and Banda enliven the pages of this otherwise austere publication. It is, therefore, not too surprising to see Charbonnier's report appearing in the April–July 1934 issue of the *Bulletin* (No. 35, pp. 20–24). This version does not include the statistical table of initiates, an unfortunate omission which weakens the article, giving it the character of one of Father Walker's fables rather than of the economic reports which make up the main body of the *Bulletin*. Nevertheless, it did attract the serious attention of the *Bibliographie ethnographique du Congo Belge,* which summarizes it in volume two as follows: "A secret society the members of which indulge in human sacrifice, drink the blood and eat the flesh of their victims, for reasons of revenge and for pleasure, doing no more in this regard than conforming to the customs of their ancestors" (p. 17). This critical bibliography does not note that it had already listed the 1925 version of the Charbonnier report that appeared in the *Recherches Congolaises,* in its first volume, where it is presented as an "important communication."[10] To my knowledge, the version appearing in the *Bulletin de l'Agence économique* attracted no further attention.

The leisurely debate continued, however, in the *Recherches Congolaises.* In 1938 some further "Réflexions sur l'homme-tigre" appeared, this time by M. Le Testu[11] in reply to Lieutenant Regondeau's contribution on that subject published in 1931. One wonders what interest this honorary chief administrator had in stubbornly rehashing a report that was by then some twenty years old. On the surface, at least, his article is nothing more than a recapitulation and an elaboration of Regondeau's point that the Charbonnier report deals with an exceptional case that is based more on superstition than reality.

[10] See p. 161.
[11] June 1938 issue, pp. 147–168.

Nevertheless, there are certain aspects of Le Testu's remarks which make one wonder whether Charbonnier's report is what it seems. In the first place, Le Testu identifies Charbonnier with Giraudoux: "Giraudoux's tiger-men," writes Le Testu, "that is to say, Charbonnier's, since he [Regondeau] declares earlier that the author [Giraudoux] reproduced the administrator's report, are not tiger-men. His little book describes only one particular case, the existence of two anthropophagous societies in a small area of the forest." Neither Regondeau nor Le Testu seems to be bothered by the exceptional presence of tigers in the Congo or by the suggestion that tiger-men are walking about in Paris. Le Testu merely remarks: "The existence of these societies was established in 1916 by the administrator Hippolyte Charbonnier. It would not seem that they had ever been spoken of before. In truth, it is the only document we have on the question." He adds that he knew Charbonnier quite well and that he was the most marvelous, the most patient, and the most sagacious investigator he had ever met. This is the first and only reference we have to H.C. as a person. In fact, this is the first time that his Christian name has appeared in print and that we can be reasonably sure of identifying him with the H.C. who published the report in the *Annales*. It is regrettable, however, that Le Testu does not see fit to enlighten us on the relationship between Charbonnier and Giraudoux. They would seem to have no more in common than the name of Hippolyte, which is also part of the full name of Jean Giraudoux.

In addition to this slight biographical information on the author of the report, Le Testu has one new idea to offer which he modestly introduces by quoting Father Feuillet, the missionary who wrote in the *Annales apostoliques des P. P. du Saint Esprit:* "Do we not see here traces of ancient sacrificial rites that have become obliterated, yet are preserved in the bosom of a secret brotherhood, which might have forgotten their meaning and kept only the profit?" To which Le Testu adds his own comment: "Profit! That is the key to the tiger-man superstition in Gabon. It is always a question of profit!"[12]

Le Testu's article came out in 1938 in the next-to-the-last issue of the *Recherches Congolaises*. The last number, which was published in 1939, contains a summary of the activities of the Society for Congolese Research, beginning with its inception on July 28, 1921, on the initiative of Julien Maigret, perpetual secretary of the organization. At the initial meeting he had read a paper on two types of fetishes common among Bassundi populations, which precipitated a discussion on the rites and practices of secret societies. Having thus revealed a remarkable singleness of purpose, the *Recherches Congolaises* discreetly ceased publication after eighteen years in the pursuit of the truth concerning the tiger-men.

The origin of this crusade against anthropophagy on which the Colonial Administration had unwittingly embarked is somewhat of a mystery. The worthy contributors to the official bulletins are lost in obscurity, but there is one name in this whole affair to which we can turn: that of Jean Giraudoux. Our primary source is *Siegfried et le Limousin,* which contains an episode relating to the genesis of *Les Hommes-tigres.* The context of the passage is the conversation between Jean and Zelten at the Café de la Rotonde where they meet for the first time since before the war. Zelten is twitting Jean about the naiveté of the French whom he sees as a peace-loving nation of small property owners who are too content with their lot to imagine the dangerous delusions of grandeur that motivate their neighbor across the Rhine. Zelten points out a number of suspicious characters right there in the café whom he knows to be spies and initiates of strange cults. He singles out in particular a blond young man reading the *New York Herald* who, says Zelten, is the author

[12] See p. 163.

of a guidebook to Europe that contains the following surprising statement: "Of all the cities on the continent, Berlin is the one that has the greatest number of anthropophagi. . . . Upwards of two hundred souls per square kilometer . . ." (pp. 36–37). The presence of cannibals in Berlin seems as likely as that of tigers in Africa, but Zelten assures Jean that it is not a laughing matter. Four years later in his rendezvous with Dagot at the Café de Cluny, Jean is to discover that Paris, too, has its share of anthropophagi. Unlike Dagot, Zelten does not produce an official report on the dangers of the secret societies he sees represented at the Rotonde. Instead he recalls an incident which Jean witnessed involving a Negro waiter called Maghéna. Jean relates the incident as follows:

> Maghéna was a Negro from Cameroun who for a few days had served at the Rotonde, in a state of incomparable stupefaction, and who had disappeared one evening between the roast and the desserts, without bringing our Beaujolais, and forever, like that Hungarian prince who was giving a dinner party, then went out on the pretext of keeping an eye on the caviar, and was never seen again, except in London, Dieppe, and Lennox. (p. 37)

Zelten, however, gives quite a different version of the disappearance of the Negro waiter:

> *You* considered Maghéna a perfect idiot who was dismissed by the proprietor. In point of fact, he was kidnapped by a group of Germans and today lives in Berlin. You may remember that, at the time, the Rotonde was all a-quiver, in a state of great excitement, which you told yourself was caused by the presence of Courteline, who came there to play his game of piquet. But Maghéna was the reason for all the passion. Just like a fledgling ephebus in New Athens, Maghéna had been brought back from the Congo by a Swiss, appropriately named Schweitzer, who had got him out of prison, where he was awaiting death as a Tigerman. He was chief of the Dibamba kettle—that is to say, the one

who handled human sacrifices for the initiatory rites of the district. I shan't tell you whom he had killed or eaten, since the victims were probably increasingly close relatives of the chief, and besides, he was not known between Gabon and Ubangi for the originality of his menus. But he was the repository of a good many hypnotic secrets, and the expression in his eyes was the most glorious distortion of light and thought that had been seen in Berlin since Lilidny. I recently paid him a visit in the hideout at Rummelsburg where his keepers starve him or gorge him with food, according to the brightness they want to give to their lighthouse. You, a model Frenchman, while the hive was in an uproar in the presence of the fetish, you were ascribing all the fuss and clamor to the fact that Courteline had just made a grand slam in no-trump without any aces. ... (pp. 37–38)

From Zelten's disconnected and enigmatic account, which only the initiated could follow, a few ideas and impressions emerge. First of all, there is the picturesque setting of the Café de la Rotonde, which was the popular gathering place for the *Bohême* of the early twentieth century. Giraudoux was frequently seen there, and it is here that Courteline reportedly wrote one of his best boulevard comedies, *La Paix chez soi* (peace in one's own house). The Rotonde was also the headquarters for a network of spies such as Mata Hari and revolutionaries such as Trotsky and Erich Mühsam. However, the conspiracy which caused so much excitement on the evening that Zelten is recalling had something to do with the unexplained disappearance of the Negro waiter from the Cameroun, who walked out on his customers in the middle of the meal without bringing the wine and the dessert. At this point, one must read between the lines to try to reconstruct what went on in the lively imaginations of some of the *habitués*. To a matter-of-fact Frenchman like Jean, the explanation was simple: the waiter Maghéna had been fired by the management for some stupid error, and the excitement

fetish, the kettle, Dibamba, the human sacrifices, and *l'homme-tigre*—suggesting that H.C.'s original article appearing in the *Annales* in 1921 was read before a group of initiates at the Rotonde. This would explain "the uproar in the hive in the presence of the fetish" and the urgent appeals in the *Recherches Congolaises* from 1922 to 1925 when the celebrated report finally appeared in the Brazzaville journal subsidized by the Colonial Administration.

At this point, one may well ask who was the creator of *l'homme-tigre*. Is Charbonnier's report based on an actual investigation of this secret society or is it a hoax? Did the colonial administrator really exist or is he, too, a fiction? Why was the report published in three different journals? And what is the role of Jean Giraudoux in this quixotic crusade?

Neither Charbonnier nor Giraudoux created the panther-man, although they may have created his existence in the Congo. The problem first arose in the British Colonies in the Sierra Leone territory where the colonial government took severe measures against an alleged society of leopard-men. In 1912–1913 a famous trial took place, which is recorded by J. K. Beatty in his book *Human Leopards* (London, 1915). According to this account, as of 1890 the native population of Sierra Leone complained that it was being decimated by cannibals. As a result of an investigation, it was discovered that the murderers belonged to a secret society of leopard-men. Between 1895 and 1912 seventeen trials were held and 186 natives were indicted for murder. However, the evidence was far from conclusive, and the most striking thing about the whole affair is the ignorance which the administrative authorities displayed of the language, customs, and mentality of the natives. Beatty supposes that these cannibalistic practices were rooted in a superstition having to do with the preservation of virility, but he has no precise information with which to substantiate his thesis. In fact, the literature available on African customs during the heyday of British and French colonialism is so very scant that Charbonnier's report is suspect by virtue of the quantity and precision of detail which it offers in this dimly defined realm of human knowledge.

Assuming that Charbonnier's report is fictional, or at best a parody of one of these trials, one is tempted to question the existence of Charbonnier himself. There was indeed a Hippolyte Charbonnier, who entered the civil service as an assistant on June 24, 1913, and who was promoted to the rank of colonial administrator on March 19, 1918. This is all we know about him, however, and he does not seem to have published anything but this report. In fact, it is far from certain that he was the author of it or that he knew anything about it. The first version of the report, which dates from 1921, is signed only with the initials H.C. followed by the title "colonial administrator." The 1925 version is presented as an "excerpt of a letter from M. Charbonnier, assistant in the Civil Service, dated Tchibanga, November 26, 1916." The *Recherches Congolaises* customarily listed its contributors by the last name only, prefacing it with M. for *Monsieur* in the absence of any other title. In 1925 there were a number of government employees by the name of Charbonnier. Unless the reader was curious enough to check back and find out which Charbonnier had the rank of assistant in 1916, the identity of the contributor to the *Recherches Congolaises* was as vague as that of the H.C. who published in the *Annales*. By the time the third version of the report appeared in 1934, Hippolyte Charbonnier was no longer listed as an employee of the Colonial Administration, which may explain why this article is signed L. Charbonnier. I was unable to determine what this new initial stood for unless it be Le Testu, who was the first and only person ever to mention the full name of Hippolyte Charbonnier, and this was not until 1938 in one of the last issues of the *Recherches Congolaises*.

It may be that this obscure administrator was really the author of a hoax that was published first in a Catholic missionary magazine, then in a colonial journal founded in Brazzaville, and finally in an official government publication, the *Bulletin de l'Agence économique de l'Afrique équatoriale*. If this is the case, Hippolyte Charbonnier deserves to be better known. For this alone, he may well go down in literary history along with Charles-Louis Philippe, Charles Andler, and the German Romantics, as an influence on Hippolyte-Jean Giraudoux. Whether we should take at its face value Giraudoux's account in *Les Hommes-tigres* of how the administrator's report came into his hands is an unanswerable question. It is significant, however, that Giraudoux does not bother to mention the fact that Dagot's letter had already been published twice before. Giraudoux certainly knew about the existence of the 1921 version, as the passage from *Siegfried et le Limousin* would indicate. It is also more than likely that he knew of the 1925 version, since at that time his office was located in the same building as the Office des Colonies. Just why he thought Charbonnier's report deserved to be published a third time and under his own distinguished name is a mystery to which he finally provided the key when he unmasked the tiger-men in *La Folle de Chaillot*.

Les Hommes-tigres is a two-pronged hoax or literary deception that is typical of the *esprit normalien;* that is to say, it represents a certain brand of wit for which the students of the École Normale Supérieure, the intellectual elite of France, were famous. There is even a word for it in French, *canular,* which is a hoax of gigantic proportions that takes in a wide range of people over a long period of time. From 1921 through 1934 Charbonnier's account of the rites and practices of a secret society of panther-men was taken seriously by Catholic missionaries, members of the colonial administration of the Congo, the economic agency of French Equatorial Africa, ethnographers and bibliographers, to say nothing of the vogue it has since had in travel books, films, and even in the dance. However, not only did the acceptance of this report make a mockery of the anthropological research of the period, but it is at the same time a political parable directed against the cannibalistic practices of capitalism.

In the preceding chapter on *La Folle de Chaillot*, I pointed out the analogy between the profiteers, who were founding a corporation to drill for oil in the subsoil of Paris, and the initiates of a secret society of cannibals in the Congo. In presenting these equally inhuman characters, Giraudoux utilized the same literary device: a dehumanized stereotype, a caricature of a nonhuman race, which has the face of an idol. "The signs by which the initiates of certain clubs or sexual perversions recognize each other are childish as compared with the way we soldiers of fortune are known to one another. A mat quality and a glimmer of death on the face . . ." (*La Folle de Chaillot,* pp. 14–15).

The analogy between the tiger-men and the profiteers goes much deeper, however, than the technique of presentation. The operations of the secret society itself bear a certain resemblance to the workings of the corporation, which is by definition a secret society, or so it would appear from the French word for the corporation, which is a *société anonyme,* a curious designation that dates from the Napoleonic *Code de Commerce.* Each society has its fetish, whether it be the panther or the golden calf; each society has its kettle, be it the *marmite* or the big bank; and the kettle is filled with the blood or money of its victims. To be initiated into these societies, a prospective member must give proof of his readiness to make human sacrifices to the power of the fetish, even if it costs the life of his next of kin. We may recall that the profiteers in *La Folle de Chaillot* all present their credentials by relating their role in a swindle which resulted in the death of innocent people.

The objectives of these secret societies are roughly the same. Charbonnier suggests that the tiger-men are merely continuing the customs of their ancestors. L'Abbé Feuillet goes a step farther and maintains that they have forgotten the meaning of such customs and are concerned only with the profit to be derived from them. Le Testu concludes that profit is the real key to the tiger-man superstition in the Congo[15] as it clearly is to the activities of the profiteers in Paris.

In a general way, then, the rites and practices of the tiger-men as well as their facial characteristics parallel those of the profiteers. There are many details, however, in Charbonnier's report that can be elucidated by certain economic facts that must have been known to Giraudoux, whose career in the diplomatic service began in the political and commercial division of the Ministry of Foreign Affairs. A convenient source of these facts for the period with which we are dealing is Lenin's *Imperialism,* which gives a well documented picture of the economic factors which led to the outbreak of World War I. Lenin's work was written in Zurich in the spring of 1916 and was first published that year in the Swiss collection *Contre le Courant.* In the preface to the first Russian edition, dated April 1917, Lenin explains that he had written the work with an eye to the tsarist censorship, so that he was forced to formulate the few necessary observations on politics in "that cursed Aesopian language, to which tsarism compelled all revolutionaries to have recourse whenever they took up their pens to write a 'legal' work." Thus, Lenin speaks of Japan when he means Russia and of Korea when he means Finland. While Lenin was composing his *Imperialism,* Charbonnier was supposedly conducting the investigation which he reported in a letter to the Colonial Administration dated November 26, 1916.

[15] See pp. 163, 165.

Assuming that Charbonnier was also using an Aesopian language, one is tempted to interpret the existence of two secret societies, one in Bouyala territory and the other in Liaba, as a reference to France and Germany. When Charbonnier limits his report to Bouyala, the territory he knows best, the implication is that he is referring to France. The statement that there are three groups of tiger-men in Bouyala territory suggests an allusion to the famous trio of Parisian banks, the Union parisienne, the Banque de Paris et des Pays-Bas, and the Société générale, which according to Lenin controlled 55 per cent of the total resources of the principal St. Petersburg banks in 1913.[16] When one recalls that it was to recover France's loss in capital, brought about by the Russian Revolution, that Clemenceau, the "Tiger," instigated the war of intervention against Russia in 1919, Charbonnier's first article in 1921 on *l'homme-tigre* takes on a new significance.

Another detail of the Charbonnier report on which Lenin's *Imperialism* throws some light is the business about the kettles. Each group of tiger-men has two kettles. The rules of the society require that an equal number of victims be provided for each kettle and that a balance be maintained among the kettles of the three groups. The two kettles may be a reference to bank and industrial capital, which were beginning to merge. In this connection, Lenin quotes Jeidels as the authority on the subject: ". . . the big banks are striving to make their industrial connection as varied and far-reaching as possible, according to the locality and branch of business, and are striving to do away with the inequalities in the local and business distribution resulting from the development of various enterprises" (p. 39).

This policy of equalization is often implemented by terrorism.

[16] "Imperialism, the Highest Stage of Capitalism," in *Imperialism and Imperialist War* (1914–1917), Vol. V of *Selected Works* (New York: International Publishers, n.d.), p. 47.

Charbonnier describes the way in which the victims are selected to keep the pot boiling:

> To feed the kettle . . . the hunt provides the victims; it is directed at people who are objects of the Society's hate, jealousy, resentment, greed, or scorn. If there is no reason, one is created; with this end in view, a few of the associates will go off to find the individual they want put to death, and will ask him, for example, to immediately lend them a large sum of money. The latter will ask for time, will say that he doesn't have that much money; they will insist and will repeat everywhere that he is a bad rich man, that they asked him a very small favor and that he refused them: the reason is created. (pp. 27–28)

The victims of the secret society may be seen as the branches or subsidiary companies which depend on the main bank. Lenin alludes to a similar practice in the banking world: "Quite often industrial and commercial circles complain of the 'terrorism' of banks. We are not surprised, for the big banks 'command' . . ." (p. 39). In other words, and as Lenin shows by the example he cites, they refuse credit to industrial enterprises that take decisions contrary to the will of the bank.

Even the details of the sacrificial rites of Charbonnier's tiger-men take on a precise meaning by analogy with such financial scandals as the Panama Canal or the Stavisky affair, not to mention the fictitious enterprise of the profiteers in *La Folle de Chaillot*. According to Charbonnier, the tiger-men cut off the victim's head, drink his blood, and eat his tongue, liver, and forearm, but the body is hacked up and scattered. "The main thing in such matters," says Charbonnier, "is to find the victim's body so as to know whether a crime or a sacrifice is involved and consequently whether one is dealing with a murderer or a secret society" (p. 38). This fine distinction could be another Aesopian reference to the difference between the bankruptcy of a free enterprise caused by the normal workings of free competition, in which case the bankruptcy is disclosed by an examination of the balance sheet; and a fraud committed by a corporation, which after having devoured the profits, conceals the sacrifice or the fraud by scattering the limbs of the body; that is to say, by carving up the enterprise into subsidiary companies. The scandal which ensues when one of these fraudulent enterprises is exposed has its parallel in the secret society of tiger-men:

> The expedition does not always succeed; it may happen that the victim manages to break loose, recognizes his aggressors, and shouts out their names. The latter try to kill him and flee; their scheme has failed; the associates agree to hush up the matter and to pay blood money, if need be, to the relatives of the deceased. If there happen to be any bothersome witnesses, their death is assured. Finally, if the matter comes before the authorities, either the accused denies everything, and it is extremely difficult to condemn him if the members of the kettle to which he belongs want to save his life, or else the accused confesses, and then one may be certain that he was obliged to do so under penalty of death by the members of the society. He will give a version of the crime that will avert suspicion and not reveal the secret. (pp. 37–38)

The mysterious operations of the banking world were particularly suspect in the eyes of Jean Giraudoux because of the feud between two powerful clans within the French government—the Berthelots and the Poincarés. Giraudoux was a protégé and admirer of Philippe Berthelot, who was, among other things, the architect of the Treaty of Versailles, and profoundly antipathetic to Poincaré, popularly known as "the wall of money." His reaction to these two families and what they stood for is portrayed in his novel *Bella* (1925), the only one of his creative works which was generally recognized to be polemical. The subject of the Berthelot-Poincaré quarrel was the failure of the Industrial Bank of China, of which André Berthelot, Philippe's brother, was one of the directors. The bank was apparently the victim of certain fluctuations of the Exchange, or perhaps of some imprudent investments, which resulted in such losses that it had to resort to a settlement in 1921 from which its rival, the Bank of China, profited.[17] The name of Berthelot was compromised in that settlement, and Poincaré managed to bring about the political downfall of his opponent in foreign affairs, Philippe Berthelot, as well as the financial ruin of his brother.[18] Poincaré's resignation following the elections of 1924 led to a decree of amnesty in April 1925, and Philippe Berthelot was recalled to the Ministry. *Bella* came out in the month of October 1925, the same year that the article on the panther-men appeared in the *Recherches Congolaises*. However, the play of forces between the two "kettles," the Bank of Indochina, which was a government institution, and the Industrial Bank of China, which had a larger capital, must have been well known in government circles long before the actual settlement in 1921 and could very well have inspired the original version of *Les Hommes-tigres*.

While the Poincaré-Berthelot quarrel in all probability accounts for the first two publications of Charbonnier's letter, why did Giraudoux enter the picture in 1926 and publish the letter under his own name? On July 23, 1926, high finance brought Poincaré back to power, and Giraudoux was relieved of his duties as Chief of Information and Press. He published *Les Hommes-tigres* in December of that year, in a limited edition and with no fanfare. The date of publication coincides with an event in the literary world which may have more significance than Poincaré's return to power in explaining Giraudoux's motivation. At this time another and more illustrious writer was travel-

---

[17] See P. Desfeuilles, *Monographies économiques* (Pierre Roger, 1927), p. 89.

[18] See Auguste Bréal, *Philippe Berthelot* (Paris: Gallimard, 1937), p. 203.

ing through the Congo, where he observed firsthand the practices of concessionary companies, which were depopulating the
districts more methodically than the secret society of tiger-men.
André Gide was profoundly shocked by the brutal use these
companies made of native labor. His reactions were reported
by Marc Chadourne in an interview published in *Nouvelles
Littéraires* on July 3, 1926, entitled "Voyage d'André Gide en
Afrique." "Have I been moving about up to now in a network
of lies?" he asked himself.[19] His much discussed book, *Voyage
au Congo,* did not come out until 1927, but this article generated
a good deal of advance publicity, stirring up indignation at the
exploitation of the natives by the big companies. Giraudoux
doubtless derived a secret pleasure at being several years ahead
of the Gidian conscience and could not resist the temptation to
publish the results of another investigation, implying that the
perpetrators of these crimes were right there in Paris.

Charbonnier's report was published a fourth time in April-
July 1934, following the Stavisky scandal, which furnished another illustration of the parable of the tiger-men. In fact, the
fable was constantly renewing itself throughout the years between the two wars. The disillusionment that followed upon
World War I, the widespread belief that wars are fought mainly
for profit and that big business is essentially predatory, the
haunting fear that Marx and Lenin might be right in maintaining that capitalism bears within itself the seeds of its own
destruction—all of this, combined with the rise of fascism and
the growing threat of another world conflict, lent an aura of
universal truth to the fiction which Giraudoux and his friends
promulgated so joyously.

As is obvious from the quotations cited here, Charbonnier's
article is of no literary interest whatsoever. It has all the terse-
ness and factual detail of an official report and could not be

[19] (Paris: Gallimard, 1927), p. 96.

farther removed from the style of a writer like Jean Giraudoux. The interest of the text lies primarily in the use which Giraudoux made of it as a symbolic image of the hidden forces that rule bourgeois society. Before Giraudoux exposed these forces in *La Folle de Chaillot,* he once more used the metaphor of the tiger in the play that electrified Europe by its prophecy that war would break out in spite of all efforts to avert it. In *La Guerre de Troie n'aura pas lieu,* appropriately entitled in the English version *Tiger at the Gates,*[20] Cassandre attributes the causes of war to destiny, which she describes as "a sleeping tiger." When asked to elucidate, she enigmatically replies that this is a metaphor addressed to young girls.[21] In 1935 Giraudoux was not yet ready to throw caution to the winds and openly attack the profit motive as the principal cause of war, preferring to cloak his thought in the striking image of the sleeping tiger.

Giraudoux had long dreamed of writing an anticapitalist comedy. Shortly after the success of *Siegfried,* when asked by a newspaper reporter what plans he had for his next play, he jokingly replied: "My dream would be to stage the letters exchanged by Lenin and Charlie Chaplin for such a long time. . . . Didn't you know? Why certainly. . . . Do tell me how you would go about getting them if you were I!"[22] It was not until the defeat of 1940, when Giraudoux sincerely believed that the end of his world had come, that he was sufficiently aroused to realize his dream and convert his earlier prank into a serious work of art.

The episode of *Les Hommes-tigres* shows that Giraudoux drew heavily upon his memories of the early 'twenties in writing *La Folle de Chaillot.* The resemblance between the prof-

---

[20] Christopher Fry, *Tiger at the Gates* (New York: Oxford University Press, 1955).

[21] *Théâtre complet,* VI, p. 12.

[22] *Paris-Midi,* May 1, 1928.

iteers and the tiger-men is only one instance of this. There are other characters in the play, such as the friends of the happy plants and animals,[23] whose identity and meaning are explained in *Siegfried et le Limousin*. The role of the Health Officer Jadin, "specialist in Gabon on the extraction of ticks," is a veiled reference to the doctor-missionary, Albert Schweitzer.[24] Likewise, the brief appearance on stage of "a dirty gentleman" is reminiscent of a play by Courteline, *Un Sale Monsieur* (1920), which dates from the time when he and Giraudoux frequented the Café de la Rotonde.[25] On the whole, *La Folle de Chaillot* seems to be a flashback to an earlier and simpler period when wars were fought strictly for profit and oil was king. This black-and-white approach to the problems of the human condition reveals a certain naiveté and a freshness of vision that sets him apart from his contemporaries. Not that Giraudoux was ever the dupe of the society he portrays with such elegance and politeness. Unlike the eighteenth-century moralists, whose relationship to their society he likens to that of a contented cuckold,[26] Giraudoux was aware of the sinister forces at work in the world. He did not confuse them, however, with the mainstream of humanity, in which he never lost faith. He simply wrote them out of the human race.

[23] See p. 148.
[24] See p. 168.
[25] See pp. 166–168.
[26] See his essay on Choderlos de Laclos, *Littérature,* p. 67.

❖ VIII ❖

Conclusion

Arthur Miller has stated that before a play is art it is a kind of psychic journalism, a mirror of its hour. "The journalistic shell of a play—its reflective mirror surface—is its mortal part without which it could not be born. But its transcendency springs from the author's blindness rather than his sight, from his having identified himself with a character or a situation rather than from his criticism of it. Thus history unveils the painful irony without which no play continues to live: that without a certain love for what he hates, without a touch of hands with his adversary, his work will not outlive its mortal frame."[1]

In relating some of Giraudoux's works to the crucial period in which he wrote, I have tried to convey the spirit of the times and the author's reaction to it. As Arthur Miller so perceptively states in this same article: ". . . nothing is harder to remember, let alone convey to a later generation than the quality of an earlier period. What finally survives when anything does are archetypal characters and relationships which can be transferred to the new period." The literary qualities of Giraudoux's theatre and the archetypal characters and relationships which he suc-

---

[1] "What Makes Plays Endure?" Thoughts prompted by the forthcoming recording of the playwright's current "A View from the Bridge." The *New York Times,* Sunday, August 15, 1965, X, 3.

ceeded in creating are obvious reasons for the survival of his plays. What is less obvious and more difficult to demonstrate is the author's involvement in the characters and situations which he describes, without which, according to Arthur Miller, no play continues to live. Giraudoux was aware of this, too. "I speak well when I have something to say. Not that I manage to say exactly what I want to say. In spite of myself, I say something entirely different. But that, I say well," he admitted in *Intermezzo*.[2]

The need to communicate a message that he dared not state clearly is the secret spring of Giraudoux's eloquence and style. It is no accident that symbol and metaphor make up the texture of that writing which eludes analysis as long as the critic persists in separating the form from the content of his works. His aesthetics and his politics are closely linked; one sets off the other. To express his ideas Giraudoux evolved a form that suited the exigencies of his thought and time.

The difficulties of Giraudoux's style are due in part to the complexity of his thought as well as to the need for discretion. Let those who find Giraudoux devious recall the heroine of *Intermezzo*, whom the author defends thus: "If evil-minded people find her complicated, it is precisely because she is sincere. Nothing is simple but hypocrisy and routine" (p. 115). Giraudoux had difficult conflicts to resolve. He had the clairvoyance of a prophet; but, as he himself stated, no one pays any attention to a prophet and one who warns that the end of the world is coming seems to be in league with those who are trying to bring it about. The only effective strategy is denunciation,[3] and as a loyal government employee, Giraudoux could not bring himself to openly denounce the leaders of his society. He was too

[2] *Théâtre complet*, IV, 72. The English version of the play is entitled *The Enchanted*. Adaptation by Maurice Valency (New York: S. French, 1950).

[3] Essay on Choderlos de Laclos, *Littérature*, p. 67.

much a part of it, too committed to a way of life which he loved as well as hated. Furthermore, clairvoyance and sincerity are not qualities which a career diplomat can display openly. Giraudoux resolved these conflicts by writing for the theatre, where he found a more active outlet for his meditations on political problems than at the Ministry of Foreign Affairs. This outlet was only partially satisfying, however, for the exigencies of the commercial theatre imposed a discipline and a discretion as rigorous as that of the diplomatic service. But within certain limits Giraudoux was able to engage in a public debate on the burning issues of his day and to carry his audience with him.

He was often accused in his lifetime of evading these issues, of being obscure, ambiguous, and inconclusive in his theatre. The spectators and the critics sensed that the playwright was treating a current problem, but unlike Arthur Miller or Edward Albee, Giraudoux rarely deigned to discuss his work or give any precise clue as to its genesis and meaning. The newspaper interviews which preceded and followed his plays rarely elicited anything more than a barbed quip or a complaint that the critics had missed the point of the play. Even at rehearsals, from which Giraudoux was able to judge the effectiveness of his work and to revise his script accordingly, the actors and directors relied more on a fleeting look or gesture on the part of the author than on any word of explanation to guide them in their interpretation of his work. In spite of the close rapport between author and director, Jouvet was no better informed than the critics as to the author's intentions.[4]

Giraudoux's extreme reserve was due in part to a certain modesty or code of behavior which was fashionable at the time. His evasion of serious discussion, his love of mystification, and his ambivalent attitude toward most controversial questions were characteristic of the company he frequented. As the world situa-

[4] See Appendix III.

tion became graver, these attitudes provided an increasingly convenient mask for his real opinions. He was not unaware of the moral responsibility he was shirking by hiding behind his mask of levity, obscurity, and courtesy. The confessions he did make in *L'Apollon de Bellac* and *Sodome et Gomorrhe* and the forthright denunciation he makes of the profiteers in *La Folle de Chaillot* lend credibility to the sentiments which he reportedly expressed to André Beucler at the time of the defeat:

> Lately we have been moving toward lies. Threatened by solutions of force, which will explode, which will take over for the praiseworthy purpose of saving the State without saving it, for it will be too late, and of recovering a national honesty without recovering it, for again it will be too late—threatened by this hard and base future, men, who have antennae and who are neither saints nor idiots, quite naturally choose the immediate profit, the black velvet mask, the "nobody is any the wiser," what we call rackets. One day we shall have to hide everything of ourselves in a crowd formed in haste: we had better go about it in advance! What I'm driving at is this—*that obscurity, as a method or an end, is also a lie, the most artful, the safest, the most modern.* It is destined to replace opportunism and will soon be superior, even on a literary level, to inner necessity, as opportunism formerly was in politics superior to dogmatism, as scheming formerly was superior to talent; and Balzac told it straight to our faces. Shortly no battlefield will be left on which to distinguish ourselves.[5]

This rambling discourse is another confession that Giraudoux was more interested in making himself heard than understood. Certainly he had no love of controversy and no taste for martyrdom. Until he no longer had anything to lose, he was not ready to stand up and be counted among the pure in heart. But perhaps the test of a great playwright is his ability to reconcile his integrity as a citizen with his integrity as an artist. History

[5] *Les Instants de Giraudoux*, p. 134. My italics.

proves the painful irony that there is a middle road which permits both the citizen and his art to survive. As a political leader, Giraudoux did not display the qualities of Louis Aragon or André Malraux, but as a dramatist he was an eloquent and sophisticated witness to the drama of his generation. He followed the course of history at first with passionate interest, later with anguish, but rarely with the cynicism that so often marked the writings of his contemporaries. When studied in their chronological order and in their historical context, his writings reveal a remarkable continuity of thought and opinion on the future of France and postwar Europe. The study I have made of the author's reactions to the victory of 1918 and the defeat of 1940 as reflected in his theatre is only a beginning. *Siegfried* and *La Folle de Chaillot* are but parentheses around his major work, which I have barely touched upon. But what does emerge from this limited study is an image of twentieth-century man which is the antithesis of those wretched, deranged, and troubled creatures who overrun the literature of our times. It is man at the highest point of bourgeois society, man who analyzes his problems with lucidity, who never gives up the battle to be master of his destiny, and who plays his role on the stage of life with irony, dignity, and eloquence, as befits a member of the human race.

❖ Appendix I ❖

The following chronology of the life of Jean Giraudoux was supplied by the Ministry of Foreign Affairs.

Born October 29, 1882.

Former student of the École Normale Supérieure.

Vice-Consul in training, in the political and commercial division of the Ministry of Foreign Affairs—June 14, 1910.

Attaché in the political and commercial division—September 15, 1912.

Vice-Consul 3rd class—September 6, 1913.

Received mention in the Ordre du Régiment—September 10, 1914.
Received mention in the Ordre de l'Armée—June 30, 1915.

Chevalier of the Legion of Honor for military service—July 31, 1915.

Received mention in the Ordre du Régiment—September 10, 1916.

Embassy Secretary 3rd class and unattached—May 15, 1919.

Reinstated—April 2, 1920.

Section head of the Services des Oeuvres françaises à l'étranger—September 18, 1921.

Secretary 2nd class—July 1, 1921.

Head of the Services des Oeuvres françaises à l'étranger—October 10, 1921.

Charged with the duties of his rank in Berlin—May 17, 1924.

Head of the Press and Information Service—October 31, 1924.

Secretary 1st class—April 5, 1925.

Officer of the Legion of Honor—January 13, 1926.

Specially employed by the Committee for the Evaluation of Allied Damages in Turkey—December 31, 1926.

Embassy counselor and continuing as specially employed—July 24, 1928.

Charged with a mission in the Prime Minister's cabinet—July 10, 1932.

Minister Plenipotentiary 2nd class and continuing as specially employed—April 26, 1933.

Reclassified in the ranks and Inspector General of Diplomatic and Consular Posts—July 1, 1934.

Commander of the Legion of Honor—July 31, 1936.

July 29, 1937, to June 16, 1940: Commissioner General of Information.

Retired November 21, 1941.

Died January 31, 1944, in Paris.

❖ Appendix II ❖

This record of the number of performances of Giraudoux's plays directed by L. Jouvet, 1928–1945, was furnished by the Théâtre de l'Athénée.*

In chronological order of first performance:	Number of performances by L. Jouvet
I — 1928 — SIEGFRIED	302
II — 1929 — AMPHITRYON	254
III — 1931 — JUDITH	61
IV — 1933 — INTERMEZZO	116
V — 1934 — TESSA	298
VI — 1935 — LA GUERRE DE TROIE N'AURA PAS LIEU	255
VII — 1935 — SUPPLEMENT AU VOYAGE DE COOK	195
VIII — 1937 — ELECTRE	183
IX — 1937 — L'IMPROMPTU DE PARIS	52
X — 1938 — CANTIQUE DES CANTIQUES (Comédie Française)	68
XI — 1939 — ONDINE	311
XII — 1942 — L'APOLLON DE MARSAC	124
XIII — 1945 — LA FOLLE DE CHAILLOT	397

* Jacques Hébertot was kind enough to inform me that 214 performances of *Sodome et Gomorrhe* were given at the Théâtre Hébertot from October 12, 1934, to May 25, 1944.

✧ Appendix III ✧

Athénée Théâtre Louis Jouvet
24, Rue Caumartin, Paris
Opera 16–45
Saturday, February 4, 1950

Madame Agnès J. Raymond
Grand Hotel de Liège
4, Rue de Liège
  Paris, IXᵉ

Madame,

  You could not have chosen a better source of information to draw upon for the preparation of your thesis on the works of JEAN GIRAUDOUX than the Bibliothèque de l'Arsenal. There you must have found all of our author's complete works for the theatre, in the Edition IDES ET CALENDES of Neuchatel, which includes the "variants."

  May I also point out to you a text of vital importance, for it is a revelation of GIRAUDOUX's character; this is "Visitations," a lecture given in Switzerland in 1942, also published by Ides et Calendes.

  The testimony you ask me to give you in an interview could not, I fear, shed any further light for you on Giraudoux, who never gave himself away. You, too, will discover him only by reading him according to your personality and your heart. I cannot yet speak of him, as I plan to do, until much later.

  With best wishes.

Sincerely yours,
/s/ Louis Jouvet.

✧ Appendix IV ✧

The following passage is reprinted from the program notes to *La Folle de Chaillot*, performance of December 19, 1945, at the Théâtre de l'Athénée.

Play in two acts
Théâtre de l'Athénée
December 19, 1945

"*La Folle de Chaillot* was performed for the first time on October 17, 1945, on the stage of the Théâtre de l'Athénée, by Louis Jouvet."

We have not been punctual.

That date, my dear Jean, which you had inscribed more than two years ago under the title of your play, we were not able to comply with.

"*La Folle de Chaillot* was performed for the first time on December 19, 1945."

We are late.

This postponement of a few weeks which we granted ourselves could be explained; the reasons that justify it are rather numerous but of no great importance. But there is another delay of which we are guilty.

This definitive precedence and anteriority in which you are now, has irremediably outdistanced us. We are late in service and devotion, in gratitude and affection. This boundless respite you have taken has suspended our emotions *in the astonishment of a revelation*.

By reason of this irreducible interval which nothing will fill and which separates us forever, here we are in deadly solitude. Surrounded by all your characters, haunted by those heroes you have given us to use and have entrusted to our care, we see our responsibilities increase, we measure our ignorance. The meaning of our occupations and gestures grows more serious. We have been slow to understand.

Now suddenly your absence awakens a precious and rare presence. *A new light illumines your writings.*[1]

In each of your works your silence creates a message which is increasingly enigmatic. Perspectives open up; conjectures come to mind. We are late.

Each of your plays anticipates, foretells, and presumes; each one affirms your prescience.

In this world of negations and shipwrecks, within these limitations in which we live, your plays bring us a belief, a faith, a taste of renewal and of grandeur.

December 19, 1945, is the first day of dress rehearsal in this new and dateless life into which you have entered. This lead that you have taken, my dear Jean, has caused a delay on our part, which can be repaired only by a continuous and unending dialogue.

Louis Jouvet

[1] My italics.

❖ Index ❖